WHITE AS SNOW

WHITE AS SNOW

Conquering Sexual Abuse and Adultery through Christ

S H E L L Y   B L A N K

WestBow
P R E S S
A DIVISION OF THOMAS NELSON

WestBow Press books may be ordered through booksellers or by contacting:

WestBow Press
A Division of Thomas Nelson
1663 Liberty Drive
Bloomington, IN 47403
www.westbowpress.com
1-(866) 928-1240

ISBN: 978-1-4497-3325-4 (sc)
ISBN: 978-1-4497-3326-1 (hc)
ISBN: 978-1-4497-3324-7 (e)

Library of Congress Control Number: 2011961720

Printed in the United States of America

WestBow Press rev. date: 01/13/2012

"The Spirit of the Sovereign LORD is on me, because the LORD has anointed me to proclaim good news to the poor. He has sent me to bind up the brokenhearted, to proclaim freedom for the captives and release from darkness for the prisoners, to proclaim the year of the LORD's favor and the day of vengeance of our God, to comfort all who mourn, and provide for those who grieve in Zion—to bestow on them a crown of beauty instead of ashes, the oil of joy instead of mourning, and a garment of praise instead of a spirit of despair. They will be called oaks of righteousness, for a planting of the LORD for the display of his splendor" (Isaiah 61:1-3, NIV).

Acknowledgments

For my husband, Russ, who would like me to put my words on the page: "To help even one woman would be worth it." Thank you for the everlasting perseverance—that of Atretes! For Janet, my faithful, loyal friend who listened beyond human capabilities and loved and served like Jesus: thanks for being my reality check. For Vicky and Paula, who sat in the rocking chair on my front porch and served, listened, cried, and encouraged: I wouldn't have made it without all of you.

And for my Creator, my healer, my Savior: "Whom have I in heaven but You? And besides You, I desire nothing on earth. My flesh and my heart may fail, But God is the strength of my heart and my portion forever . . . But as for me, the nearness of God is my good; I have made the Lord God my refuge" (Psalm 73:25-26, 28a, NASB).

Introduction

I once was given seven minutes to write down the names of all the villains, heroes, turning points, and successes in my life—each on a sticky note. Next I had to put them in chronological order. Finally, I had to analyze them, looking for any lies that might have taken root from those events and people during the course of my life—"lies" meaning anything that is not a biblical truth. This group exercise was designed to help develop a biblical worldview, as opposed to one that merely filters all life experiences through a secular worldview—the world's viewpoint. It was a powerful exercise.

I found myself focusing on mainly the villains in my life—wolves, as I have come to call them. I had plenty of painful experiences listed as well. After analyzing them, we were asked to share one lie with our group. I didn't want to share the really dark, painful stuff in such a public format, so I shared something I felt was pretty generic: when I was thirteen, my family was asked to leave our church. It was actually a profound event in my life, leaving me feeling I'd never really measure up to the expectations of good Christians. I understood and knew that this belief was a lie, but I realized that in my heart, I actually still believed it. I also began to realize that this, such a fundamental fracture in my sense of truth, was only the tip of the iceberg. I was actually carrying around quite a collection of lies I'd accumulated throughout my life—many of which had taken deep roots. To really find them, I had to start at the beginning, and I had to finally come to terms with the wolves in my life.

*   *   *

When I look at pictures of myself as a little girl, I see a smiling, blonde, pudgy-cheeked little angel. It's funny how I grew up feeling the opposite. I wonder how a person can look one way on the outside and feel moldy on the inside. Brown eyes, big grin, dimples on my little girl hands—and whenever I compared myself, no matter where I went, I felt somehow less than the freckled, fair-haired children I stood next to.

This is my story of hope and healing. In order to understand my recovery, though, first you have to know how it all began— where I came from and how I got myself in so deep. In my story, perhaps you'll find a bit of your own.

If you are a Christian, you may find this book to be very comforting. I hope it communicates a message of freedom.

If you are not a Christian, you may think I am letting all the wolves out there off the hook. What I am hoping you find is that I am. Read on.

"Look I am sending you out as sheep among wolves. Be wary as snakes and harmless as doves" (Matthew 10:16, NLT).

WOLF #1

"For you created my inmost being; you knit me together in my mother's womb . . . How precious to me are our thoughts, O God! How vast is the sum of them! Were I to count them, they would outnumber the grains of sand" (Psalm 139:13, 17-18a, NIV).

In many ways, my life started out very normally—whatever that is. I did a lot of happy little kid things and had a lot of good people in my life. Being a Montana girl, I lived in a "safe" neighborhood where I had a lot of freedom to roam. My best pal, Janet, lived next door. We took full advantage of that freedom, curiously exploring the nooks and crannies of our neighborhood every chance we had. We did a lot of investigating, and when we couldn't find anything good, we made stuff up.

Janet had big brown eyes; pale, perfect skin; full cheeks; and short, dark brown hair. She was adorable and painfully quiet, but the kind of kid you'd want to pick up and squeeze and tickle. I was her blonde sidekick; I had dimples and brown eyes and was the more outgoing of the two. We were each the youngest in our families, so we were used to either a lot of attention or none at all as everyone got busy doing the things older people do.

Some of the adults on our block seemed fascinated by the two of us and were instantly friendly. Some neighbors ignored us or shooed us out of their backyards, while others welcomed the curious explorers. We eventually gained quite the reputation for snooping and for carrying out our various antics.

We became friends with an older couple down the street, Mr. and Mrs. Doves, when we were preschoolers. We visited them often. Actually, we just thought their house was intriguing. We were curious to see inside. They also had a beautiful teenaged daughter whom we admired and likened to a modern-day princess. Their home was much different than each of ours, as they only had one child. It was quiet, immaculate, and each of them was very patient with us as we shared our stories and asked all sorts of questions about their home and family. They tolerated us well.

There were other areas we explored as well. It always seemed we had a vast expanse of territory to roam and concoct our imaginary world in. In actuality, however, we had only four blocks. We ruled our little kingdom, though. Our school, Bitterroot Elementary, was just around the corner from our houses, which enabled us to identify every square inch of that building from the outside. We knew every neighbor, their children, and most pets between us and our school. Walking to school each day, we passed two ferocious beastlike dogs who nearly always tried to attack us from behind their tall wooden fence. We never actually saw them, but we knew they were gigantic, slobbering monsters with huge fangs. We walked faster as we went by the white fence, hoping *this* would not be the day they actually broke through the old slats.

We also explored Pumpkin Creek, which ran past the end of our street. For a year, we had another friend, Mari, who lived right next to the creek. Mari was from Finland. She was very different from us. She had no television, her toys were different than our typical fare of dolls and small cars, and her house smelled different. She even ate different kinds of food. She also had a younger brother.

We were at a loss for several months as to how to communicate with her, as she did not speak much English. We, being from rural Montana, obviously did not speak Finnish. Gradually, however, we learned to communicate well enough and developed a relationship. Mari soon joined us in our adventures. The three of us often traveled up and down the creek bed, trying to catch water skippers and trying to stay in or out of the mud, depending on our moods.

One year the creek flooded. Our whole neighborhood had to work together to sandbag around houses and the street. It was a crisis that brought people out of their homes even more than usual. I was a quirky kid who liked the energy of the near disaster and the togetherness that resulted from all of the grown-ups united, working for a common cause. Mari's family actually got to know a lot of people during that time.

We had to go past the creek to get to the public pool—the happening place during the summer months. At twenty-five cents a visit, we went often and swam until our feet looked like white raisins. When it was time to leave, I'd be so hungry my insides would ache. The three-block trek home seemed to take forever. Occasionally, one of our other friends might share a single pretzel from a bag she purchased at the vending machine. That nibble just made my hunger pangs worse. I remember resenting her as I watched her eat the rest of the bag herself.

All kinds of things happened at the public pool. On a pretty regular basis, the pool had to be emptied for the token brown substance found at the bottom of the shallow end. Sometimes it was a chocolate bar, and unfortunately, sometimes it wasn't. Once I was held under by an older boy until I began to see stars. That had a lasting effect. After all my mom and dad spent on swimming lessons, I still cannot swim the crawl for fear of putting my face in the water. I remember when a girl slipped off the top of the high dive and landed on the pavement. Although I was there, I never really found out what happened to her. Rumor had it, she died. A lot of my life was lived out and defined at that pool, but I had other hangouts, too.

There was a giant weeping willow in Janet's front yard. Its branches were so strong and flexible that we could stand on them, bouncing from the top of the tree to the ground. We played in it for hours at a time, transforming it with our imaginations into a giant ship or a house. Inside the branches of that tree we felt completely invisible, sheltered from the rest of the world—maybe even safe.

Janet and I investigated all items of interest in our territory, and we were sure that was exactly why the neighbors on our street kept their front yards clear of anything interesting. I suppose we really had no sense of personal boundaries in that regard. Anything was up for grabs. We were so thorough we even knew what was in nearly everybody's backyard.

We knew the nice neighbors who didn't mind our nosy behavior. We also knew the mean neighbors who'd kick us out of their front yard simply for opening up mysterious containers or tiny doors laid in their brickwork. We were very famous— infamous, really—for our behavior, especially with our parents. When we were really young, our moms had to keep a tight watch over us or we'd strip down to our birthday suits in the backyard and roam free. As we grew older, we were more likely to dare each other to eat dog food or pick the neighbors' prized flowers.

*   *   *

Eventually we had another friend—a boy. Carter hung out with us and played lots of girl games. He never complained. There were no other boys around, so I figure he had the "If you can't beat 'em, join 'em" attitude. Carter had an amazing imagination. When we girls ran out of ideas, he'd come up with a new one. He had an older sister, but she, like the rest of the older kids who lived on our block, usually ignored us. Carter, Janet, and I were the youngest, but we seemed to cause the most trouble. Mari was also included. We three girls dragged poor Carter around, forcing him to be the prince or the pirate in all of our games. Many times he found himself dressed up with all the girls—high heels included.

It was our team mission to spy on all the neighbors, and when necessary, our older siblings. We were not above crawling beneath cars to wait for teenagers to get in and make out. We played in everyone's front yard, climbed all the trees that were accessible, determined both my house and Janet's were haunted, and let our imaginations run wild. One summer, we made some older kids angry by tattling on them—our house ended up being flooded with a garden hose while my family was out of town. When nothing much was going on, we made up stories. And we had slumber parties.

Slumber parties were a mixture of fun, fear, love and hate, pillows and PJs, and lots of giggling. I dreaded the ghost stories Janet's older sister told, but I loved feeling included. I hated being the first to fall asleep and the only one up at the crack of dawn.

Slumber parties happened frequently, although never at my house. We played games like Light as a Feather, Stiff as a Board. Chanting those mystical words, we'd magically lift a person up into the air. Playing with the Magic 8 Ball or the Ouija board, all we really conjured up were our own giggles and screams. Once we got to sleep out in Janet's camper, which led to a night of exploration all around the neighborhood and beyond in our nightgowns and bare feet. Our territory grew as we did. Thankfully, we all arrived back to the camper safely.

Although we weren't completely without parental boundaries, the fact is, it was Montana in the seventies. There wasn't much danger to be found. Our parents guided us but trusted our neighbors and the safe history of the community to help raise their children. We weren't aware of many unsafe happenings in our wintry little cocoon. We just took care of each other. We were completely naïve.

We usually steered clear of the only known dangerous neighbors—the Rodneys. Their kids were the toughest on our street and in our schools. There were a lot of them, and frankly, you just never knew when something was going to happen at the Rodneys'. Janet and I had, of course, been over to their house and witnessed a terrible fight between the father, mother, and oldest son. It included physical blows, a lot of screaming, and eventually an ambulance and police officers. After that, we rarely visited, but we couldn't help but be intrigued by the way the family seemed to implode, explode, inhale, repair, move along, and begin the cycle all over again with some new drama.

Sundays were always a trial for me—no cartoons on and no sisters or brothers young enough to play with, and Janet was unavailable. She went to a different church and had to hang out with her family all morning. So I'd play on my own, grudgingly, and wait until it was time to head off to church. I did a lot of waiting, actually. I was an early riser from the time I came out of the womb, apparently. I remember calling Janet's house early one Saturday morning. I was up, and my parents were still sleeping. When Janet's mom answered, I knew it was early—too early. Her mom informed me that Janet was still asleep and requested I "please wait to call until later in the morning." I remember going back to our Lazy Boy recliner, curling up in my blanket, and waiting.

*   *   *

I really was pretty cute when I was little. As a toddler, I had curly, blonde, shiny hair; chubby legs; and a perfect little dimple. All the pictures I have of myself from when I was a toddler speak *cute*. Those cute days abruptly ended when my mom got a hold of the scissors, though. In a flash, I was transformed into what today looks like a boy in frilly, lacy dresses—although if I am completely honest, the haircut was my idea. I wanted my hair to look like Janet's. It didn't quite work for me like it did her.

Through the elementary school years, my school photos say it all. In one particular photo, I have a very nice mullet-style haircut. I say "nice" because I wore a big, goofy smile which makes me think I either didn't care how I looked or thought I was lookin' good. I lean toward the second option, but I don't like to admit it. To complete the ensemble, I wore a giant turtleneck and homemade bell bottoms. I don't blame my mother for my bad haircuts. I remember distinctly asking her to cut my hair—hence all the bad photos. I actually don't remember being disenchanted with my hair until later in life when it took two hours to style. Those were the big hair days of the eighties. Still, what I see now, when I look at all those photos, is just a little girl. It's funny how you can look at a person and think you understand her. You can even talk to her, listen to her, laugh with her, carry on a friendship with her for years, and actually never quite know her—especially if she is a person like me. But bad hair was probably the least of my troubles. By the time I started to care about that, I'd already begun to feel the real aches of this world. The veneer of my innocence had not only cracked, but also had nearly shattered.

I learned about death pretty young. One day after school, Carter came to my house and asked me to come with him to his house. He was confused; he couldn't seem to wake up his mother. Janet joined us along the way, and when we got to Carter's house, he led us to his mother's bedside. There she was, not moving. I remember her distinctly having a grayish pallor about her, and I remember one of us reaching out and touching her. I remember Carter being very confused. We decided to get help, and when we did, we learned that she was dead. In fact, his mother had died in her sleep the night before, but no one knew it, because everyone had just gotten up and ready for work or school and left. Janet and I went back to our own mothers. Carter never could again. It was a sobering awakening to the harsh realities of this life. It's funny how I never saw a change in Carter, though—other than not seeing him for a while. His life was dramatically altered forever, yet the rest of the neighborhood just went on, the same as usual.

Carter's dad hired a housekeeper to help with meals and cleaning. She looked like Flo from Mel's Diner, and I remember being afraid of her. She was short, direct, and didn't seem to like us hanging around. Eventually Carter, his sister, and his dad moved out of the neighborhood. A chapter in my childhood concluded, and another began.

*   *   *

I was very young when I met my first wolf. I am not talking about Little Red Riding Hood, although I think I dressed up as her for Halloween one year. I am talking about a real human being who acted like a wolf. My parents sent me out on my way, much like Little Red, into an environment that they trusted—Granny's house (a trailer, really). Actually, I went there a lot to spend the night.

During the day, I remember walking around in the yard outside her trailer, catching grasshoppers as big as my hand. Without close siblings, I never had any playmates at family functions. I remember being very bored while I waited for all the adults to get finished talking and leave so that I could have some time with Granny.

I have two older sisters. I also have older cousins. One cousin began paying particular attention to me whenever I stayed with Granny. Through particular circumstances, he actually wound up living with her. My visits with her were fun during the day, but at night, she would go to bed, and I would sleep on the couch alone. My older cousin invariably wound up coming out to the couch to "watch TV." It turned out to be more than watching re-runs of Godzilla. I was very young. It was very confusing for me—frightening, but exciting. He made me touch him, and he touched me. As a child, I didn't understand that it was wrong to be playing games of this sort with my cousin until one night when another cousin walked in on us.

The cousin who caught us lived just across the street from Granny's with his parents, my aunt and uncle. He yelled at my cousin to knock it off, but it felt like he was yelling at me. I realized for the first time that what we had been doing was wrong. Instantly I felt dirty. I felt guilty and responsible. Somehow I had allowed it to happen; it was somehow my fault. I owned it. At my very young age, I felt unworthy, damaged, and disconnected. I had no way of expressing it. The lies were planted and quickly became part of my identity. I not only *felt* dirty and damaged, but I also *was* dirty and damaged.

I tried to tell my parents what was happening, but in that day and age, parents just didn't have the resources to handle it. My wolf went on to torment me, and in my mind, I became a very lost sheep, piecing together a web of coping strategies that would entangle me for many years to come.

I took a lot of baths when I was little. I loved bath time. What an escape: warm water, bath toys, bubbles, and the hope that I would be clean! I remember a time when my mom came in just at the end of my bath and, putting her hands on her hips, she stared at my legs, accusing me of not scrubbing my dirty knees. No matter how hard I scrubbed, I couldn't get them clean. That too seemed somehow fitting. The lies had grown—roots spreading wider and wider, entangling my heart—and no one knew. No one could help me chop them down and clean them out.

Soon after, the giant weeping willow that had cocooned Janet and I, as well as most of the other children on our block for so many years in our play and imagination had to be cut down. Our kingdom of safety came crashing down around our houses. For a day our two, front yards were nothing but a mass of tree parts, branches, and roots. We were buried in the mess of that tree that had been so dear to all of us. I was angry that no one had consulted us. Even after it was explained that the roots were invading the water system and causing damage to the sewer system on our block, I was resentful. After all of the branches were cleared, I remember the wide-open space—a grotesque vacancy. Yet somehow I could identify with the emptiness left behind. Sadly, it seemed fitting. Another chapter in my childhood had ended.

Dear Heavenly Lord your Holy Spirit makes intercession for the weak. Hear our cry, O Lord,

Why have you allowed this to happen? Why, when you say you love us, would you allow this thing to happen? Why her—and then, why not her? Someone else? Would we ask this of anyone? Won't you set this child free—this child who cannot speak for herself? Protect her. Teach the ones who love her to protect her. Teach her that she is still yours. Teach her that she is still pure. Set her free from the pain and the memories—the memories that will follow her the rest of her life. How will she forgive if not for you? If she doesn't, how will she live—in bitterness? In fear? Teach her that she is still worthwhile—still yours.

Teacher, free the wolf. Help him who is controlled by his desires. Help set the one free who is controlled by your enemy. This wolf is not the boy/man you made him to be. Set him free from his path. Help him to choose freedom. Amen.

Be comforted

"In the same way, the Spirit helps us in our weakness. We do not know what we ought to pray for, but the Spirit himself intercedes for us with groans that words cannot express" (Romans 8:26, NIV).

Discussion Questions

1. What was your fondest memory growing up?
2. Did you always feel protected as a child?
3. Can you name the people you were closest to in your childhood? How did they define your upbringing?
4. Are you able to detect biblical truths or worldly lies that may have developed in your childhood? Take a look at what the Bible says about our worldview and our worth (Ephesians 2:10, 2 Corinthians 5:16-17, 1 Peter 2:9).
5. Can you write or discuss a time when you felt unprotected? Does this pertain to physical or sexual abuse? What feelings are unearthed when you bring up this part of your life? Are you able to label those emotions?

WOLF #2

"God is our refuge and our strength; an ever-present help in times of trouble. Therefore we will not fear, though the earth give way" (Psalm 46:1-2a, NIV).

I hated middle school. It was a terrible thing for a girl with a bad haircut, shifting hormones, and a genuine lack of academic interest to endure. Being forced into an environment with other hormonally-challenged adolescents and teachers who dressed like the Bee Gees seemed barely survivable. I felt like I was in a fog of emotions most of the time, and my academic performance reflected that.

I had many rather curious teachers who made life at least interesting, if not downright scary at times. One teacher, after many failed attempts at band class instruction, actually threw a student head-first into one of the lunchroom garbage cans. Another teacher took the time to make up nicknames for each of us. Strangely enough, he gave me the name Clear Woman. As nothing was very clear to me at all in those middle school years, it somehow felt encouraging—even endearing. Another teacher never actually had a conversation with any of us all year. He just waited for us to shuffle in to our seats, and then he'd commence his lecture until the bell rang. It was in his lab that I first dissected a frog, a pig, and a shark. Someone ate the eyeball of the frog, but Mr. Stone never missed a beat. He just kept on talking! I often found myself staring at the glossy, bald spot on top of his head, intrigued by the reflection cast from the windows. Did I mention I lacked any substantial academic interest? Actually, the entire middle school exercise was a painful endurance.

Socially, I was very interested in school, but I was not one of the popular girls. Gretchen was the most popular girl. Coincidentally, she was also mean. She invited people to slumber parties and waited for the first girl to fall asleep. Then she'd pour warm water over the girl's hand and make fun of her if she wet the bed. To top it off, she'd tell everyone about it at school on Monday. I wonder why girls liked her. She did have nice clothes (no homemade bell bottoms), and she was really funny—as long as you weren't on the receiving end of her jokes. She made life miserable for many of us during sixth and seventh grade, and then she moved away. In her wake, other girls filled the "most popular" role, and I was established by eighth grade as a sort of quasi-popular girl.

I was, at least briefly, a member of the middle school drill team, cheerleading squad, volleyball team, and track team. I tried basketball but was a complete failure, never understanding exactly where the key was and too afraid to ask for clarification. My track career ended as soon as it started. I ran one race, got second place, and decided I hated the adrenaline rush leading up to the start, so I quit.

I developed crushes on a few boys . . . and one teacher. He dressed like Andy Gibb from the Bee Gees, complete with gold chains, chest hair, and a perm. That was actually pretty cool back then. I had that crush until the day he yelled at me in front of the whole class for coloring my entire left hand blue. After that, I was just mortified every time I saw him. I think that's when my negative self-talk began; I started telling myself that I was really stupid. Of course, when one colors oneself blue, one does have to really wonder.

*   *   *

I had a crush on a boy named Gator. Gator had the cutest smile in the world. Every time I saw Gator, my insides would get warm, and I would forget how to talk. He once told me I was sexy. Interestingly enough, at the time, I didn't even know what sex was. I must have said something to my mom about Gator, because I came home one day after school to find a book on my bed about sex. It came complete with diagrams and definitions. I read it cover to cover. It may have been the only book I read in middle school.

It was about that time when my family was asked to leave our church. That was extremely upsetting to me, as by that time, church had provided the one social group that I felt safe in. No one picked on me there, and I had a few friends who were nice. I longed to grow up to be in the high school youth group. There were cute boys there, too, and they all did fun things together like going on ski retreats, singing, and acting out skits—at least it sounded fun, even though I didn't ski or sing, and I had never been in a skit.

When my parents left that church, we never returned to it. I had been Nazarene. I was saved at church camp and again several times after that. I believed that every time I sinned, I needed to get saved again. I said I believed that God had died for me and that I was forgiven until I would mess up again. I tried to clean up on the outside, never understanding that what Jesus really desired was my whole heart. Why would anyone desire what was on the inside? Who was I anyway? I was a dizzy, silly kid with bad haircuts and homemade clothes who did strange things like coloring her hand blue. I was confused a lot. I thought catch-up work had something to do with ketchup. I misunderstood my teachers, forgot homework, lost things, and didn't really care about what my teachers would blather on about in front of the class. I had lots of labels for myself at this age, and none of them were very glamorous, intelligent, or pure. I got saved a lot. I sinned a lot.

I entered high school with visions of *Grease* dancing in my head. I desperately wanted to be Sandy—to be saved by the handsome prince who would drop everything he loved for me. I wanted to be valued—perfect—like Sandy. Unfortunately, I couldn't sing, and if I was completely honest with myself, deep down I wanted to be a Pink Lady. I related to the Pink Lady side of the tracks. The Sandy lifestyle seemed boring. I was angry at being given minor boundaries, and I was daring—a dangerous combination for any young woman.

My priority list, if I had one, contained items pertaining to boys, clothes, music, and friends. Janet went on to high school with me. We had shared lots of childhood memories together, and in our freshman year of high school, we made more memories— only not so innocent. We had lots of Pink Lady moments—minus the pink coat, which was kind of a bummer. I secretly thought those were really cool.

There wasn't a lot to do on the weekends. We didn't have a culturally diverse community or even a cultural repertoire in our small town. Very few kids had hobbies outside school. School was the social web of the day. Kids made up the culture. The fall schedule consisted of football games, parties, and keggers. Then in the winter, it consisted of basketball games, parties, and more keggers. In the spring, we planned for prom, went to prom, went to parties, and camped out at the keggers.

During my freshman year, I met an older boy who took a serious interest in me. At first I wasn't prepared and didn't like the attention. Then I realized the social benefits of having an older boyfriend. I started dating him and soon fell head-over-heels for my first love. When things began to get physical, I had a stark memory of the events from my early childhood with my cousin. It was almost like a veil that had been drawn over my eyes was suddenly thrown open. I was vividly aware of what had gone on. I remember telling my first love about these horrible experiences, and fortunately, he was mature enough to encourage me to tell my parents.

Again, talking to my parents didn't really help. Help came in the form of lots of talking. Everyone talked about the problem for a few months, and then we all hoped it would just get better or go away. Yep, going away is what I became a master of saying and doing. To make my bad memories go away, I shut them out. I practiced telling myself, "When life hurts, just shut it out, and it'll go away." That was another lie to add to my growing collection. I sought refuge in all the wrong places, like that country song, "Lookin' for Love." That was me. I wanted—craved—healing and protection. Above all, I wanted the one true love of my life. I needed protection, but I didn't really know it, and I don't know if I would have allowed it. Protection was not something I would have said out loud that I wanted. If the truth had been told, I don't know if I would have been able to identify with that emotion or label it. It's like what every little girl wants—to be held, cared for, cherished . . . protected. But you don't say it out loud; it's just there. Many little girls have it. I did not. This was not through the choice or the intention of my dad and mom, just through the circumstances of the world I was in—a broken world filled with wolves. Because I didn't have it, my heart ran wild. I chased the things I thought would bring relief, and I liked the thrill of being bad—even with the repercussions. I wanted to see how many bad things I could do to see if anyone really cared enough to stop me.

I hurt so much on the inside. I think I really wanted other people to know how much I hurt over the fact that I felt often, that all I was worth was what I could give or accomplish. I wanted to let people know that it hurt to feel that my only value was in my ability to please a man sexually, too. Why else would a sixteen-year-old race someone down a winding mountainous road driving in the wrong lane? Why else would a sixteen-year-old take a detour, driving all the way to Seattle (an eight-hour drive) with only her best friend and without her parents' permission? Why else would a sixteen-year-old search at such a young age for her true love so desperately and recklessly?

*　　*　　*

I kept dating the potential Mr. Right, and he would turn out to be Mr. Wrong. I dated one boy who actually asked me to marry him the first time we met. He was really rich. I liked the idea of having a swimming pool, a chef (because I only knew how to make canned soup and French toast), a jet, and really nice cars. We dated sporadically throughout high school, and then it more or less fizzled. We met later on in my senior year one night—a night that turned out to be one of the most devastating nights of my life.

I never had a curfew. My parents suggested times that I should be home. They asked me to call if there was a problem, and they trusted me to do that. I was pretty upfront with them about where I was and what I was doing. That awful night, I brought the rich boy home, and while my parents slept, we began to get physical in my basement. He took hold of my neck with his teeth and never let go. I cried out silently, and when it was over, he just looked at me and smiled. He knew I would never tell—and I didn't.

He was wolf number two.

Father God,

Do you see this girl? Does anybody see her? Her heart is broken. She doesn't even know which way to turn. Her pain is turning inward. She is shutting you down and shutting you out. She is shutting the door on everyone she loves. She feels this is the only way to control the feelings inside. She is drowning. Can't you help her—send someone to her?

Set the wolf free. Help him to see the path of destruction he has laid before him. Help him repent. Do not let him be a coward. This is not who you designed. This is a monster.

Why, Lord? Where is this path leading? Amen.

Comfort

"The LORD is my rock, my fortress, and my savior; my God is my rock, in whom I find protection. He is my shield, the power that saves me, and my place of safety" (Psalm 18:2, NLT).

Discussion Questions

1. Do you believe boundaries are important for children? What were your boundaries?
2. Do you have any memories from your childhood—especially your teen years—which really stand out? How have those memories impacted your life and belief system? Did anything happen that you felt you could never tell?
3. Did you ever identify with a main character from a movie growing up? Describe that character.
4. What kinds of self-talk (negative and positive) do you participate in? Read Philippians 4:4-8. How does this impact some of your current patterns?
5. What is the main battle going on within the main character? Do you identify with the emotions of wanting to know if anyone cares deeply enough for you to rescue you? Have you ever tested people intentionally to determine your value?

WOLF #3

"Be strong and courageous. Do not be afraid or terrified because of them, for the LORD your God goes with you; he will never leave you nor forsake you" (Deuteronomy 31:6, NIV).

Promises are sometimes really hard to keep. I promised myself to be home earlier on the weekends. I promised myself I would spend more time with my parents. I promised myself I would not get any more parking tickets. I promised myself I would be a better girl. I promised myself I would clean my room again . . . better . . . even if it was already spotless.

I promised my sisters I would try harder. They each tried to reach out to me in their own ways—shopping or having lunch with me. Neither produced much result. Both of them were busy raising young children, and they didn't seem to have much energy or resolve to help a struggling teenager. At one point, I made the careless remark that my sister, while pregnant, looked like a fat cow. My words seem to have made a lasting impression on her, while her words of advice just bounced off of me. The truth is, I was embarrassed by their lack of cool—something that was definitely important to me at the time. I assumed they didn't or wouldn't understand me. They were so "pure" and had never made mistakes. They had never pushed the envelope with my parents. They were good girls. I was not. My perceptions were warped. As a result, I felt I often disappointed them. I lashed out at them instead of reaching out.

I promised to try harder in school. I promised my dad I would not get any more parking tickets. I promised to go to the cabin with my parents when they went, but when the time came, there was always something better to do in town. And my parents began allowing me to stay home on the weekends alone, so I promised my friends that I would have a party. And that was one promise I kept.

*   *   *

High school parties can get out of control in a hurry. Mine did, but I have to say, I did nothing to control it. I spent a lot of time preparing for it, but I didn't really think the whole thing through. As far as high school parties go, this one could probably go down in the history books as being one of the biggest in our small town. My party started with kids from each of the four different classes in our high school, enough alcohol to intoxicate Mexico (I still don't know where it all came from), outdoor garbage cans filled with Long Island Iced Teas, dancing upstairs and down, and plenty of loud music. It ended with a visit by the police, teenagers running rampant through our backyard, and my principal showing up at the door to take his daughter and me home with him. I refused to comply.

When I saw the mess left in the morning, I felt used and sad that I had allowed my parents' home to be treated in such a way. There was chewing tobacco plastered on our front door, broken panels of stained glass, a large section of fencing destroyed, alcohol stains on our carpet, stolen cassette tapes, and just the regular huge mess a house is left in after such an out-of-control party. I also felt empty, lost, and alone. Truthfully, I was a brazen, uncaring, self-absorbed, guilt-ridden young woman. I was trapped in my own path of self-destruction. But I was just getting started.

Disgusted, I promised myself I would not drink another wine cooler—another promise soon to be broken. My friend called me and asked me to come over. He wanted to watch movies on his new VCR and drink wine coolers—an offer just too hard to pass up. Watching movies on a VCR was kind of a new thing. A machine that allowed a person to watch a favorite movie over and over whenever they wanted was a brilliant invention! So talking to him on my rotary-dial telephone, I agreed to come over. I put my new cassette tape in my new car and headed off for another adventure.

The 80s was an electrifying time. We suddenly had a lot of new technology at our fingertips, and it was all very enticing—Walkmans, boom boxes, and hair crimpers. Also new to us were music videos and personal computers. The day "Thriller" came out on MTV, we planned a world premiere party around it. We memorized the dance routine and worshipped Michael Jackson. It was a whole new world—all very exciting.

The friend I was going to meet was actually a guy I'd been friends with since my freshman year. He was at his brother's apartment. His brother was older—actually out of high school—but I didn't think anything of it. To me, it was just something to do. I didn't like this guy like a boyfriend; he was mainly just a guy to hang out with—and he had that VCR. There was a time when he had insinuated that he would like to be more than friends, but I had let him know it wasn't like that for me. He seemed to be fine with that. Oh, and he was rich, which helped also in my shallow estimation.

I realize now that I liked guys with money. He drove a nice sports car and knew how to check if a diamond was real. He had checked one for me that another boyfriend had given me—real! He liked to talk, which wasn't that common for high school boys. He seemed to have a brotherly interest in me and my ongoing guy problems. He also had access, via his older brother, to alcohol.

*   *   *

At a young age, I tasted lots of different alcoholic beverages, including all the beer labels bearing different animals, some "hard stuff" like MD 20/20, and sadly, wine coolers, which during that time, were a relatively new phenomenon. An older guy friend also introduced me to a mixed drink called a Tom Collins. It was interesting that no one in my family drank, yet my own palette was expanding. In my family, we had had an occasional bottle of Blue Nun with dinner at Christmas or Easter, but because drinking was a sin in our church and for other various reasons, no one drank much. Maybe that's why this forbidden fruit was so intriguing to me—that, and it was something to do.

I was a lightweight. I always wanted to be one of those tough Montana girls who could drink a cowboy under the table, but I wasn't. I also had visions in my head of being a ski bum who drank beers in the bar after skiing all day while reminiscing about the great runs of the day. The problem was that I didn't know how to ski, and I didn't know any real cowboys. The one time I went skiing in high school, I had to sit on my rump and slide down the face of the mountain to get to the bottom. I had decided to bypass the bunny slope and head right to the chair. I could and did drink, though. I was used to having a few, which meant more than two and less than ten. More than two meant I was having a really good time. Less than ten meant I was gone.

My husband's family drinks; they all handle it just fine. No one is an alcoholic. No one relies on it heavily except during large, extended family get-togethers. No one views it as a sin. Therefore, it has been an interesting contrast with my family. For my husband's family, drinking is purely a social thing. In my family, there is alcoholism. It destroyed my uncle and nearly destroyed two of my aunts. It is a prevalent and real thing. My parents had always warned me that I could take one drink and be lost to it forever. I listened but had to find out for myself how I would be with it.

I am not an alcoholic, but I have certainly used alcohol as a means of escape—much like with the family get-togethers, but on a deeper level. While I often used it to get through painful circumstances, thankfully I can walk away from it, not drink, and be fine now. I caution my own children about alcohol, as I have seen what it can do to people who cannot control it. I have seen what it can do when used as an escape, and I have seen what it can do in an unsafe situation.

* * *

The night I met my friend to watch movies on the VCR, I drank a wine cooler. I didn't even drink all of it—I think maybe half. I don't remember what movie was on. I don't even know if we used the high-priced VCR. All I know of that night is that I woke up in the bathtub with nothing on. I know my friend and his older brother were there. I don't know anything else. I woke up, and he (my friend) tried to comfort me. I just wanted to get out of there, but I was very groggy. It took me a long time to get my clothes on and then longer still to feel like I could drive home safely. I didn't understand what had happened. I didn't understand for a long time. In fact, it wasn't until much later in high school (when I learned what his older brother had done to one of my friends) that I realized what had probably been done to me.

I have tried to remember. The memory isn't there. I've had snapshots in my memory, but I don't even know if they are real. Perhaps it would be too painful to remember. I do know what it felt like to wake up naked and alone. I was embarrassed—humiliated, mortified. I blamed myself for getting sick or drinking too much. I didn't understand. I blamed myself. I owned it. I looked at it as one more episode in a very sad pattern that was clearly developing in my life. I didn't even know what a date rape drug was until my friend told me of her physical and emotional pain after a similar experience our senior year. My VCR night with wolf number three happened my sophomore year.

Heavenly Father!

I cry out to you! My words are not enough. I cannot express the depth of her shame. I ask you to set her free. She begs for love, and this is what she gets? She needs your water of life. Help her to get to it. Put someone in her path who will help set her free. Steady her aching heart. Ease her pain when she realizes the wrong done here. Surround her with your love.

Set the wolf free. Make the truth known. Do not let him fear the truth. Do not let him go on living with the guilt of his actions. Set him free. Help him to see you clearly. Amen.

Comfort

"But you, O LORD, are a shield around me; you are my glory, the one who holds my head high" (Psalm 3:3, NLT).

Discussion Questions

1. What behavioral and emotional patterns do you see developing in the main character? Have you ever developed any similar patterns? Why do some people handle trauma differently?

2. If you saw a young person beginning a path similar to this one, how do you think you could help? Would you help? Do you think she would accept help?

3. Why do you think promises were an issue? What rules did the main character establish for herself?

4. Do you see someone to blame at this point in the main character's life? Who is protecting her? Read Psalm 119. Record your thoughts.

5. Have you ever had an experience that felt beyond your control—where you felt helpless? Describe your feelings about that experience. Feelings are important to recognize. Be sure to look at each one.

WOLF #4

"'Come now, let's settle this,' says the LORD. 'Though your sins are like scarlet, I will make them as white as snow'" (Isaiah 1:18, NLT).

When I was a sophomore in high school, I was forbidden to ride on a motorcycle. My friend, Kent, got a motorcycle. Kent always wanted me to go for a ride with him on his motorcycle. Without my parents' knowledge, we took a trip to Kalispell on his motorcycle to visit one of our friends from middle school. I trusted Kent's driving after that trip—apparently more than I trusted my parents' (especially my dad's) advice.

My dad was and is a very quiet man. I would have to say he just may be *the* quiet man. After all, he lived with his wife and three daughters. We probably talked more than he ever realized was humanly possible, especially after being raised with all brothers. He is patient, generous, and gentle. When I was a kid, he took me fishing every Saturday morning the fishing pond was open. I really loved watching for the bobber to go up and down—my signal that I'd caught one. I loved that time with him. He also took me hunting one time. My feet became so frozen that he put them inside his shirt, directly on his belly, to get them warm. We also hand-delivered his insurance calendars together on Christmas Eve day—without fail—for several years. I remember sitting together in the old suburban one particularly snowy Christmas Eve. I knew we were late getting home for the evening's festivities, but I wanted those moments with the giant snowflakes falling to last with him.

It was hard to disappoint my dad. It was also hard to disappoint my mom. As my years in high school advanced, though, it seemed like I was becoming a master at it. My mom was sweet and quirky. All my high school friends liked my mom. We'd often come up to my house on the hill just to hang out with my mom. She'd tell funny stories and listen to ours. Then we'd gossip about high school stuff, and she'd fill us in on the daily soap opera scandals. Our house was cozy, cluttered, and welcoming. My mom contributed heavily to the welcoming part. I often found myself—even in high school—coming home and sitting on my mom's lap to chat. She handled me with a great deal of patience. My sisters were another story, though.

Being twelve and fifteen years older than your baby sister must give a person a certain feeling of latitude. In fact, now that I am an adult, I realize that with age comes life skills and knowledge that I didn't have as a teenager. As a teenager, I often felt that I had not one, but three mothers. It wasn't wrong, just different. One sister had a lot of patience with me, and the other . . . not so much. I think they both felt I had too many privileges, and I took advantage of those privileges. It was probably (most likely) true.

* * *

I was given a monthly allowance. I drove a new car. I had a credit card for gas. I had my own cute little pink bathroom and a walk-in closet. What more could a girl ask for? Oh, no curfew—just the request to let my parents know where I was. I did hold up that end of the bargain. I dated whomever I wanted and wore pretty nice clothes. I had advanced out of the homemade category and actually made it on the fashion board at a local department store.

The fashion board not only gave me a discount on expensive labels, but also gave me a certain amount of high school prestige. The members of the teen fashion board were trained how to model, still-model, and pose, and we were given lessons on poise and manners. I remember having to put my poise into effect while still-modeling one Saturday afternoon in the mall.

I was part of a winter ski apparel scene. They had gone all-out and had snowmobiles and skis brought in. We wore ski attire, cool hats, gloves, and goggles, but we also had our faces painted with neon (it was the '80s!) sunblock. I sat on the snowmobile for my still-modeling part—perfectly posed and still. A little boy climbed up on the snowmobile and proceeded to stick his finger up my nose. With as much of a poised sixteen-year-old manner as I could muster, I gently and slowly turned my head to look at him. Instead of calmly alerting him to the fact that I was real, I in fact totally freaked him out and made him cry. His parents thought I was horrible, but at least his finger was out of my nose.

I was on the high school drill team, too. The drill team was at one time—when my sisters were in high school—quite an honor to be involved in. When I got to high school after years of looking forward to wearing those glittery, sequined uniforms and go-go boots, the drill team had started to lose its flavor, though. It wasn't the prestigious group it once had been, and the strict requirements were starting to loosen a bit. Flying splits still had to be performed at try-outs, but gone were the days of hair being pulled back into tidy little buns. We performed at football games and in parades.

I remember when the zipper on one of my go-go boots broke during a football game. At one point, when kicking, my boot sailed off into the stands. I had two flags to take care of, though, and the show had to go on. I just kept marching with only one boot on. It wasn't long after that event that my drill team days ended. I simply became too cool to be part of that dying entity.

*   *   *

Inside, I struggled with what I thought was normal teenage stuff. I wanted to be a good girl. I believed in God, but it seemed more and more like God was like a mystical version of Santa

Claus. I felt like he was only there when I *really, really* needed Him. And always I felt him threatening to leave me if I didn't behave. I had been told to follow many rules. I felt I was a rule-breaker by nature, and I believed my actions separated me from God on a daily basis. Feeling hopelessly defeated on the inside, I chose to tackle life on the outside in dangerous and daring ways.

At sixteen, I found myself on the back of Kent's motorcycle again, but this time, he was driving way too fast, and I realized way too late that he'd had too much to drink. His driving wasn't at all typical, and I just knew we were headed for trouble. We went off the road driving somewhere between 60 and 70 mph. Wearing Kent's leather jacket, helmet, and my own Lawman jeans, I flew through the air, landing bottom-first. I cracked one vertebra and compressed another. The pain in my back was comparable to having a steel rod placed midway through your spine without pain medication. However, when the ambulance arrived, my only concern was that my dad would find out that I'd been on a motorcycle. I didn't want to once again be the source of his disappointment. Even though he had never said I was, I had convinced myself that I was. I was a rule-breaker, and this proved once again how truly disappointing I could be.

As the paramedics strapped my head to the backboard, I begged them not to tell my parents. They politely ignored me. Coupled with that, I learned that the ER staff was actually considering cutting of my precious Lawman jeans! That nearly sent me over the edge—sadly, almost as much as the pain in my lower back. I hate to admit the shallow state of my mind, but it was true. I valued things as much as or more than the terrible wreck my body was in.

My parents arrived. Their general state was one of calm alarm. I believe they were disappointed and concerned. In the middle of all the pain I was in, I forgot to be afraid of getting into trouble. My parents never said they were disappointed—just relieved that it hadn't been worse. More than anything, they looked sad. They must have decided I had enough natural consequences that I didn't need a punishment, because I don't recall being in trouble.

Eventually—corset, cast, and all—I was sent home for a six-week rest. This actually proved to be a rather surprising adventure.

On the evening of the accident, I was supposed to have a date later that night with a guy I had recently met at a wedding reception—a really nice guy. It turns out that having a broken back can do wonders for your dating life! However, all dates were off for a while except with an old family friend who was also a pastor. This pastor-friend came bearing the gift: *War and Peace*. Really—a sixteen-year-old who hangs on Madonna's recent quotes in *Rolling Stone* and sports a David Lee Roth poster in her bedroom closet is going to curl up with a thousand-page book called *War and Peace*? Maybe—but not me. I was barely coherent when he asked, "If you had died last night, would you have gone to heaven?" *Absolutely not!* my mind retaliated, but my mouth said, "Yes." He patted me on the shoulder and left me feeling adrift once again.

The nice guy showed up on my doorstep sporting a college letterman's jacket in the middle of my recovery. I had called him a few days after that first missed date to explain. My parents didn't even flinch as he walked in, but my mom predicted later that this would be the man I'd someday marry; she said she knew it the moment he walked in. The nice guy's name was Russ. I tried to feel and look as attractive as possible in my corset, back brace, and clumsy white wrist cast while sitting in my pajamas in my parents' bed, worried that I hadn't brushed my teeth and annoyed that my parents kept chiming in on our conversation from their recliners in the room next door. This was our first date. Russ just sat and visited with me and flashed his cute smile. It turns out that he would be the guy I married, but that story is for later. We couldn't car date, but he came to visit often, and eventually my parents arrived at the notion that my homebound era was at an end. Dating resumed.

Russ and I went on all kinds of good, clean, fun dates. We met at the top of the hill and watched the fair fireworks together. We talked for hours after meeting on a nearby golf course at night to look out over the city lights. We watched movies. I really enjoyed his company. We were very attracted to each other, but Russ was uncomfortable with our age difference. He was in college, and I was still in high school. He was surprised at the fact that I had no curfew and stated as much. Eventually, as the summer wore on, Russ called things off. He felt it was wrong for us to date and told me to wait until I was in college. At the time we met, I was sixteen, and he was twenty. In my mind, it was just frustrating. I liked him so much that I felt it was possible and even right for us to date. He was adamant, showing the vast difference in our maturity levels.

Russ and I kept in touch over the next few months and then year. We remained good friends—always with an element of guarded attraction. Talking with Russ was like picking up with an old friend right where we had left off. I had always wanted an older brother, like my friend Janet had. I had always wanted someone to speak wisdom into my heart about life and guys. Russ served as a quasi-mentor/brother. I often took him store-bought cookies and sometimes groceries, as I was shocked at the lack of sustenance in his kitchen—nothing or just cans of soup! On these visits, I'd be reminded to enjoy my friends in high school and wait until college to date. Our conversations usually worked their way around to warning me about the guy I was dating and telling me to get rid of whoever it was. I did not listen.

I dated a lot: jocks, druggies, bad boys, good boys . . . no one stuck. As I got older, I met older guys. I wound up running into Russ at a party where I was to meet another guy—a college guy. It was awkward. Russ left. I continued seeing this guy and hanging out at his house, where we'd often watch movies or have parties with his roommates. I brought my friends, too. There was always beer, drinking, and a lot of girls filtering through. I don't know why that didn't send up a red flag—or maybe it did, but unfortunately it was more important to feel included and popular. College Guy was kind of aloof, but I thought he was really cute, smart, and athletic. He was also very interested in music, which was about all we really had in common. Once when we were hanging out at his place, the previous boyfriend who had helped me share my story about my cousin showed up. He wasn't happy to see me hanging out there. I should have listened, but I just kept pursuing.

One night, there was a huge party at College Guy's house. I got really tired and laid down in his bed, away from all the noise. I fell sound asleep. When I awoke, I discovered him having sex with me. Almost instantly, my mind concluded that my body and my brain—who I was essentially—were really only good for one thing. There was a physical part of me that felt dirty. It was so real that I felt I could have carved it out. I felt that I had somehow invited this, as I had never discouraged it. I had never said, "Oh, by the way, when I am sleeping and I am unaware of what's going on, you cannot have sex with me." I had not set many boundaries, if any. I assumed the men and women around me would be decent and respectable and follow the rules. Why I would assume that when I broke the rules continually myself, I do not know, but I hoped for it. I longed for it. I longed to be protected—cherished. I longed for the ultimate love affair—to feel clean and whole and be unafraid. Perhaps I was my own worst enemy.

*   *   *

Mean girls can make life miserable. I was plagued by a tribe of them after my involvement with College Guy. It was mainly due to the fact that he had begun dating me and called off his involvement with one girl in particular—the typical high-school-girl-scorned scenario. Although she was still in high school, she was older than me. It became a barely tolerable daily drama that persisted until a few months after I stopped going to his house, which was after that night. The damage had been done, though, and my reputation had been tainted—not that I had encouraged a great reputation. After this change in the social venue in high school, I did not make it on the varsity cheerleading squad. All my friends did. I was cast out of that inner circle. I was alone, and for the first time since middle school, unpopular.

I spent hours on my bathroom floor, staring at my wrists, wondering if I was brave enough to slit just one. I wasn't. I wondered about the devastation it would cause my family. I felt selfish, and I was in that regard. I tried to talk things through with my mom or sisters. I didn't feel like I had anyone to turn to. It was just too embarrassing to share the extent of what I viewed as my own failure. I felt I'd be judged as I had been by others—by my family. After all, my antics—parties, rude comments, failures to perform appropriately—were a continual source of jokes at family functions. Even though their remarks may not have been intentionally harmful, they drove a wedge between me and the rest of the family. On top of that, I keenly defined myself as the black sheep—the Prodigal Son. I had a visual image in my head of who I was and who my family was. No one else had apparently made the same mistakes I was prone to making. No one drank, no one had premarital sex, and no one rode motorcycles or even got parking tickets! I, on the other hand, had a particular gift for trouble. My family seemed to make light of it, teasing me for my wayward ways and bad hairdos. Yes, bad ('80s) hair had carried over into another stage of my life. Unbeknownst to my family, I was boiling over on the inside. I may have looked the part of the belligerent, could-care-less teenager, but on the inside, I did care. I cared a lot. I wanted to be just as protected, loved, and valuable as my sisters apparently had been. But I didn't feel I would ever measure up.

Determined to make the best of it, I turned to a new girlfriend who walked a bit on the wild side and a new high school—which led, unfortunately, to more drama. There were two high schools in my town. Although my parents wouldn't let me attend the other high school, I began dating a guy and developing other relationships with kids from the other school. I stayed steady with my new friends and new boyfriend throughout my senior year— only to find out the next summer that my boyfriend had been cheating on me for most of our relationship. After that betrayal, I decided there weren't a lot of guys—or people, really—who were trustworthy. I continued searching nevertheless. I closed a part of my heart.

I made another new friend—a girl who was also from the other high school. She went to a Catholic church. I started attending with her, enjoying the comfort in the strange rituals. I somehow felt better about myself after attending a service. Still, I knew I didn't really fit in and felt a bit like an intruder—an outcast. When I was supposed to say things like, "Peace be with you," I would say, "Amen." I wondered when I would ever fit in, feel clean, or be wanted for who I was.

Heavenly Father,
    Make a way for her. Make her path straight. Strengthen
her, as her journey will be long.
    Set the wolf free from his guilt and shame, O Lord. Show
him your light, and set him free.
    Strengthen the one you see will be hers. Amen.

Comfort

"But God demonstrates his own love for us in this: While we were still sinners, Christ died for us" (Romans 5:8, NIV).

Discussion Questions

1. What does the main character truly want? Is it even possible for her? Take a look at what the Bible says (2 Corinthians 5:17-19, Philippians 4:4-8, Hebrews10:19-23, Romans 8:26-27, Matthew 10:29-31, Romans 8:37-39). Can you name some things you want?
3. Who protected you in your upbringing? Who protects you now?
4. Why do some women demand justice while others remain silent regarding rape or trauma such as this?
5. Have you or anyone you have known experienced this kind of trauma? How did that person cope? How did it work out for him or her?
6. Can you give your feelings about your experiences to God and let Him take care of them? Can you pour out your feelings to God? Do you feel He listens/cares?

CHASING THE DREAM

"He will make your innocence as clear as the dawn, and the justice of your cause will shine like the noonday sun" (Psalm 37:6, NLT).

Russ and I ran into each other on our college campus. He asked me out again almost immediately. We became inseparable from that point on. He took me to church—the same Catholic church that my friend attended. I remember being especially impressed as he stepped out in the aisle to wait for me to go ahead of him to take communion. I still didn't know what to say when I received the biscuit, but Russ didn't care. The smallest things were the most endearing to me. He made me feel it was okay to just be me.

I was so overwhelmed by the fact that Russ loved me and wanted me—only me—that I didn't care what anyone said. I was convinced that Russ was going to make all things right. I got into college, and we could finally date. However, Russ was nearing graduation, and I was just beginning my education. I enrolled as a dance major, thinking that I would someday teach dance lessons and own my own studio, but it was a halfhearted goal. I was more interested in earning my degree in Russ, or Marriage Ed. After all, Russ and I had known each other for three and a half years by this time. We loved each other. We both felt we were completely compatible. I knew Russ was the man I wanted to marry.

At that time in my life, I moved from one minute to the next and based everything on my feelings—what I felt was the right thing to do. I had no idea that God had a plan for me or that I should consult him about something like marriage. I had been saved in fourth grade at church camp but obviously remained an infant as a Christian. My view was finite, tiny—inward. I know now that God's view is infinite, complex—complete. I had a lot to learn.

I told Russ I wasn't messing around anymore with guys. I was either all in or I was out. I was tired of waiting for him and for what I thought our life would be. I wanted to be married. I was sure it would bring about positive changes and a real sense of security. First I knew we had to clear the air on all of our garbage. I wanted to make sure Russ knew what he was getting himself into.

Honestly, I half expected Russ to call everything off once he knew everything. That's why, when we decided to clear the air, we went to a local bar; ordered shots of Tequila, salt, and lime; and trudged through the baggage that we each had. I shared every painful detail, and so did he. We felt that this would set us free from any future surprises. I never wanted his friends to know more than me. I never wanted to be the last to know about any of the details of Russ' personal life and previous relationships, and neither did he. I wanted to know that I was accepted. I was. We were totally free with each other, and that was a strong way for us to begin. At least our intentions were good, and we were trying to be smart about things. But we were in for a real roller coaster ride. How could we know then that we'd have years of barely hanging onto our seats and being scared out of our wits sprinkled with brief moments of laughter and fun that we'd desperately cling to? The first few years of our marriage—and on into the early stages of parenting—we really struggled. Then again, what marriage doesn't have its struggles?

*   *   *

Everyone in my family married young, but still, our families were somewhat surprised by our marriage. Russ and I were engaged for two and a half months and married in July. I was nineteen. We found ourselves immersed in an adult world that we weren't ready for—at least I sure wasn't. For years, we didn't even know any other married couples our own age. And unfortunately, Russ had a lot to teach me about just daily living. I didn't know how to cook beyond a can of soup and French toast, and it was a real struggle for me to adjust to the meager income. Suddenly, I didn't have a new car. I didn't have a monthly allowance or a credit card. I didn't have a walk-in closet, and I couldn't afford to get a perm. We didn't really have anything but the desire to be together and find our own way.

While our role models were traditional (both our parents had remained married), our ideal image of marriage was based more on the Hollywood version of love and romance. But the reality was that just getting along day after day was often a chore. Still, we were absolutely, stubbornly committed to our cause. We were going to make the dream happen.

Russ got a job in a variety of places those first few years. I dropped out of college and worked in various health clubs to supplement our income. He tried selling insurance, working for a local credit union, and then worked for Coca-Cola, which took us to Gillette, Wyoming. I was pregnant when we moved there and pregnant when we returned. Our short stint in Gillette convinced us that we both wanted to be teachers. We set goals to finish our degrees and returned to Montana. We began parenting, and Russ returned to college to earn an endorsement in education. While he was going to school, we managed the apartments we lived in, and I became a nanny for a local lawyer. I took care of our first child, Austin, while taking care of Jay, an infant, as well. I was in a little over my head, but my mother and Russ saw me through the beginning stages of motherhood. Caring for Austin and Jay was essentially like having twins without the nighttime dual feedings. It was crazy and stressful, yet we thought we were happy as we worked toward our dreams. We were developing a dangerous pattern of self-reliance, though.

Our son, Austin, was a joy from the moment he was born. He was busy but calm. He never cried except for one time that I could really pinpoint. He had golden blonde hair and said things like "Daddy-doll" for basketball. He made my transition into motherhood kinder and gentler than perhaps he had to. I had no idea what I was doing, but he made me believe my hands were capable. I wanted to be better for him.

* * *

During this time, Russ and I tried various churches. We tried the Nazarene church. With Russ's background, that was out of the question. It reminded him just a little too much of the televangelists he had seen on TV. He was totally uncomfortable there. So we attended a different local Catholic church that was a little more liberal to suit both our needs. Religion was something that Russ didn't feel comfortable talking about. It was a private thing, mostly. For me, church was good, because it meant I got to feel some hope during the short homily, and we got to go out for breakfast afterwards. I was still the outcast, however. I could only hope that someday I would fit in. I went to the Catholic church secretary and asked about beginning the process of conversion.

It was arranged that I would begin weekly meetings with a nun. I met with her one time and had so many questions about why I had to meet with a priest to receive forgiveness and why I couldn't use birth control that she told me I was better off waiting until I was really ready to become Catholic. Red flag—outcast.

A few years into our marriage, I really began to flounder. Amidst all the other struggles, I struggled with sex. I still felt that a large piece of me was dirty. I wanted it out—the dirty piece. I tried to talk it through with Russ. He wanted nothing more than to solve it for me, which I found impossible. I wound up visiting with our old pastor from the Nazarene church on and off for a while. It helped put a Band-Aid on the wound, but the wound was still festering below the surface. I still felt dirty.

I had been trying to grow closer to God, thinking my efforts should be in some way productive. I did turn to God, and I felt comfort in that. I trusted that God would handle certain aspects of our lives, especially in times of trouble. We wanted to have a second child, for instance, and didn't get pregnant right away. Then when I became pregnant, I was certain that it was a girl. We visited the OB-GYN and found that he was having trouble detecting a heartbeat with each ultrasound. We went back for more visits, and he explained that the fetus was apparently not naturally miscarrying and that they would need to perform a D&C to "clean out" the fetus. He said it was normal and actually fairly common. I was very sad; I was sure it was a girl. I was sure about this baby being the little sister I had prayed about having for Austin. I felt very sure about this baby, yet there was no heartbeat. The morning of the scheduled procedure, I prayed that God would help me through. I was scared, and so was Russ. We went in, and we discussed the procedure again with the Doctor. I explained again my hesitancy, and he said to give me peace of mind he would perform one last ultrasound. That was the first time we heard our daughter's heartbeat—loud and clear! I was pretty sure God had something to do with that.

*   *   *

Kadie was born, and then we moved right away. Russ got a job in Idaho, and we jumped on it. We were anxious for a fresh start, and Russ had promised that we would return to Montana after a few years. I knew no one. He knew just a few people. I had never had to make new friends, and I wasn't very good at it. We fumbled our way through our first couple or two and finally made some real friends we both enjoyed. The key, we discovered, was that we both had to like both people, and they had to like kids. We had no other expectations or parameters.

Russ's job was all-encompassing, as he taught, coached three sports, and ran the school store and all the concessions. He was a busy man. He would practically fall through the front door each night, hoping for peace and quiet. I anxiously awaited his return each day, wanting to talk. I needed adult interaction. The extent of mine was talking to moms and dads as they dropped off or picked up their kids from our house for childcare.

I went with Russ to all of the games, many concessions, and trips he would take for his high school organization. Russ often became frazzled, as I constantly asked him about his day and what had happened at work. I'd ask him to take us out to dinner—even on our little income—so that I could get a break. I knew it was financially irresponsible, but I was desperate for a mental break from the confines of our little house. During those years, we spent every Christmas and every summer vacation at his family cabin in Montana. We took trips back and forth to my parents' house too, but any real vacation was spent at the cabin. The cabin, although wonderful in itself and on a beautiful secluded lake, was very remote and not exactly stimulating for a young mother who needed to develop friendships back home and a break from feeling cooped up. But still, I did learn to deeply appreciate the cabin, my mother-in-law, family visits . . . and even cooking.

In those early years, I was extremely sleep—and companionship-deprived until I met our neighbor, Ann. Ann was a true gift from God. She was a pastor's wife, and I, being the ultimate buffoon at friend-seeking, called her to ask if she sold Mary Kay. It made sense to me because her skin was so clear. She didn't sell Mary Kay, but we did become instant friends in that first conversation. I started a book club not long after that and developed more friendships. Ann joined, and soon we discovered we were kindred spirits in many ways. At last I felt I'd established some real friendships and had some relief from the endless loneliness.

Eventually, I returned to school, determined to finish my degree. Of course, I still ran the daycare and the home, and my husband ran ragged right next to me. About that time, we lost

Russ's dad and had our third child, Philip. It was a tremendously busy time with no sign of relief in sight.

* * *

Philip was the cutest baby in the history of the world. I dreamed about him and caring for him like I had with my other children. I only wanted to do it better this time, as I had more experience as a mom.

Philip came to us in the middle of struggle of losing Russ's dad, and he struggled himself. He wouldn't eat and had trouble going to the bathroom. He came out sideways and hand-first. I was out of shape and out of energy. With a new baby and all the other responsibilities I had, something just had to give. I dropped out of school for a time and took care of Philip so that he could get on track. We needed to get me through school, however, so my period of rest was short. Philip went into daycare while I was in school, which I felt very guilty about. When I was home, I was running the daycare, studying, or taking care of my family and household. I felt frenzied. I was supposed to be better at parenting, but my parenting was put to the test, as I had too much on my plate. It certainly wasn't ideal—not what I had dreamed of. It was not the Norman Rockwell picture of family—more like a family in a circus. When I would answer the phone, I would often say, "Grand Central Station!" We were on a roller coaster train.

Our debt-to-income ratio was increasing on the debt side, which was increasing our level of stress. It seemed impossible to ever catch up. We kept putting one foot in front of the other and then had to take steps backward and sideways just to make it. To live on one teacher's salary with three children could be economically feasible, but not with my spending habits and my husband's spontaneity. When Russ's dad died, he dealt with it by purchasing a new Dodge truck—one like his dad had always wanted. We decided we just had to have more income.

Russ applied and was accepted to a master's degree fellowship program, which would allow him to get his master's degree for free, eventually increasing his salary. This was very important to us, but it meant spending six weeks of the next three summers apart.

While Russ was gone in the summer time, the kids and I visited my parents and Russ's mom. Traveling, eating out, and shopping were all fun but expensive. I also went to summer school and hired my nieces to become nannies for me during the summer months to help with the kids, which brought more expense.

It felt like we were working toward our goals. It felt like progress, like we were closing the gap—getting closer to the dream—even though we had to take some detours and make some sacrifices along the way. Little did we know that the biggest detour of our lives was yet to come.

Father God,

Take charge of this family. Take root in their hearts. Give them a firm footing—a house on the rock. Help them to turn to you—the only firm foundation. Strengthen them for what is to come. Protect their precious little ones; hide them in you.

If it is possible, turn the wolf away. Lead him to your truth.
Amen

Comfort

"When Jesus heard this, he told them, 'Healthy people don't need a doctor—sick people do. I have come to call not those who think they are righteous, but those who know they are sinners" (Mark 2:17 NLT).

Discussion Questions

1. Has there ever been a time in your life when you felt like you were on a roller coaster riding up and up, and then sailing down with no time for faith or God? Describe that time.
2. What role has family/friendships played in developing your faith/values? How have these relationships defined your faith?
3. Has there been a period in your life where you thought you had things figured out? Describe this time.
4. Are you ever tempted to just ignore a painful experience and not deal with its impact on your life?
5. What things/people do you rely on for strength?

AN UNSEEN PREDATOR

"The enemy boasted, 'I will chase them and catch up with them. I will plunder them and consume them. I will flash my sword; my powerful hand will destroy them'" (Exodus 15:9, NLT).

You know the part of the story where the villain enters the scene, and he is introduced: "Boys and girls, the big, bad wolf was following Little Red Riding Hood as she walked on her way to her grandmother's house. She had a basket of goodies she was going to give to her grandmother. She didn't know the wolf was following her . . ." I didn't know the wolf was following our family—beginning to encircle us. This wolf could not be seen with human eyes. And this time, I had a family.

My family got involved in Ann's church and learned a lot about the Bible. We developed a friendship with Ann and her husband Joe, which was like family. Their kids were like our kids, and our kids were like theirs. They only lived one door away from us, so I would often call Ann and ask what she was cooking for dinner, and then we would eat together on the spur of the moment. We shared everything—especially laughter and God. I thought I was really starting to get what it meant to be a Christian.

I was so pleased to see that my husband was finally willing to try a non-denominational church. I was convinced that Russ needed to change. In fact, I was sure that we would be happy if he would just come to know the Lord. Russ and Joe were buddies. They got along well, and I remember resting finally in the knowledge that God did indeed have a plan in all that was happening.

I read *In His Steps* for our book club and decided that our life was too good—too easy. In fact, I was convinced that I needed more trials to get to know Christ better. I prayed for more trials. I don't recommend asking God for trials. Soon after, Joe lost his job, and his family had to move to California. Right before my eyes, our friends who were helping so much to draw us to God left. I wondered what in the heck God's plan was then. My daughter was left without her best buddies, and my heart was broken from missing my kindred-spirit friend.

My husband was not the friend I had in Ann. He only briefly had the patience for my silly girl talk. He was often fun and friendly with our friends, but he closed off from me like a brick wall when it came to talking about matters of the heart. I felt a certain part of him was separate from me—inaccessible. I prayed about it. I nagged like a dripping faucet. I whined. I coaxed and cajoled. I grew silent. I hoped. And then I started to see something else come out in him: anger.

*　　*　　*

Russ and I moved to a new house—a bigger one in a quiet, heavily treed neighborhood. We didn't think we could get into it. Actually, we were short about $5,000, but a friend at work gave me a check for that amount and said we could have it and pay it back when we could. We went to closing and found that an error had been made by exactly $5,000. This was like God speaking to me about the house. I had asked him to make it clear to us whether we should buy it, and this felt like an answer. We were able to go back to my friend with a check for that exact amount of money that same week. We bought an extra lot so that eventually we would be able to sell it and clear some debt that was plaguing us.

Russ and I were not on the same page financially, though. As time wore on, we began arguing and fighting over finances constantly. I grew more and more fearful of spending money for the reaction I would get from Russ. His harshness shut me down. I kept praying for him to change, not seeing that I might do better to focus on myself.

I had finished school, gotten a good job, and was earning as much as I could. I taught reading and learned as much as I could about reading instruction. I felt my expertise expanding. I taught in a highly socioeconomically disadvantaged school. It was very stressful. I longed to be closer to home after school. It wasn't that far away but far enough to make me feel like I needed to be there after school to keep tabs on my kids. I would rush home, get the kids settled in, and start dinner—and then I'd run. I started running to help wash out the day's stress. I could turn my brain off, and instead of spending an hour venting with Russ about things at work, I would come in feeling more refreshed and less like I needed to verbally vomit.

Running was never a word in my vocabulary until later in life. I ran a little here and there when we were first married and after I had Kadie, and then I fell out of shape. After Ann and Joe moved away, we found new friendships, but one couple in particular helped to define the life we would eventually lead after our inevitable marital collapse. Roy and Janet were runners. I admired their physicality. I admired their marriage. They really seemed to have it together.

I admired Janet's strength and talked over my feelings of guilt about working and being a mom. Janet would agree about our friendship. It did not start off as easily as mine had with Ann. It grew to be a bond that was as strong a—or stronger—that family in many ways. Janet was not the kindred-spirit friend like Ann but more of an honest, open, fun-loving friend. We were opposites in many ways: I was sensitive and nostalgic, and she was candid and more direct—not insensitive, just not one to mull things over too long. We were both loyal, and consequently, we shared lots of laughs once we got to know one another. Our children were all essentially the same age, just each spread out by one year. When we got together, everyone had a friend. We spent vacations together; read the same books; started attending a new church together; talked over God, wine, and children; and helped each other with moves, work, and cooking. No one had been there for us-apart from Ann and Joe and our families—like Roy and Janet.

Janet, Russ, and Roy all encouraged me to apply for jobs closer to home. When a reading specialist job opened up at our neighborhood elementary school, I thought I had it nailed. I prayed and asked God to help me. I applied for that and a first-grade position but was given neither. My job was still very stressful, and I had been there long enough that I thought a change of venue would be appropriate and good. Apparently, God and I weren't on the same page. I took this shut-down pretty hard and began moving toward other goals: a marathon, National Board Certification, and my master's degree. At the same time, I moved from my reading specialist position to the classroom.

I was given a classroom of twenty-seven delightful children in the first year. I thought I was crazy. It proved to be even more challenging than I had expected with seven children on particular behavior plans. The next year, I had a reprieve from the behaviors, but the next year I was back up to nine behavior plans—one with a full-time aide. That year proved to be the most challenging of my entire life. I thank God every day that I had Christian friends at work and Janet to call upon.

Some days, the children just seemed to be crazy. I'd get one calmed down, and I'd notice another one under a table. My management skills were honed in dramatically, but even that was not enough on some days with one child who needed medication for severe behavioral issues. I'd find her locking herself in her locker or hiding under my desk! Despite all of that, when she was on her medication, I was able to see the calm child she could be, and I fell in love with her. After all, that little girl, crying out for help, reminded me of myself.

* * *

In the meantime, my husband was at the boiling point with my spending. I tried to control it, but it seemed like we just could barely get by paycheck to paycheck even though we were making more money than ever before. I blamed him in my heart for not adhering to God's Word about tithing, yet I couldn't stop buying groceries for our family and the growing crowd of friends at our doorstep. I loved to cook, provide, and entertain.

My focus shifted to more attainable goals. I began training for a marathon, which took time away from family. I worked on my National Board Certification, which involved writing every morning at 2:00 or 3:00 a.m. for nearly six months and then performing related tasks at work to complete the certification. Then I got accepted to a master's fellowship program that took me away from home for six weeks for two different summers. I grew more and more independent and farther away from Russ and God.

Every time Russ and I would fight, I would quietly give up. I wouldn't retaliate anymore. I stopped caring. I cared about my children and the home that we provided, but I couldn't take the yelling, fear, or eggshells I walked on with him anymore. I felt afraid, and even though he had never hit me, I was afraid that physical retaliation might start at any point. I had seen it a time or two when he lashed out at our boys. I wanted to protect them from harm, so I became quiet, and I really tried to control my spending. I tried not to aggravate Russ in any way. I tried to satisfy him in the bedroom. I felt like if we had sex, he was happier. He was just closed off from me intimately, and I didn't know how to reach him.

Although we had many happy times with friends—and even with each other—it was like we were headed downward on a spiraling train. I was merely waiting to crash. At times, I actually longed for a crash, but I didn't want anyone to be hurt. I hated that Russ didn't feel that way. He seemed content—even happy. How could that be? He would escape to work outside, which would drive me to work out my frustrations training for a marathon alone. I hated that he seemed oblivious to my pain. I gave up asking God to change him. I hated that I had to keep asking. I hated listening to sermons that spoke about the role of the spiritual leader in the household. Where was he? I hated waiting for the leader to protect me and our children. I couldn't breach his wall. I gave up trying. I hated myself for my selfish, inescapable feelings. I was too tired and too weak to even have hope. Little did I know that I was being taken down by an unseen predator.

When a wolf hunts, it chases its prey with relentless ambition until the prey is too tired and weak to go any further. When a wolf attacks its prey, it surrounds the prey with the many members of its family and goes in for the kill. The wolf tears at the flesh of its prey with its teeth and claws until it is able to grab a hold of the neck and break it, ending the life of the victim.

Heavenly Father,
Do not let her go astray. Do not let her become lazy or tired. Let her remember the special gifts you have given—seen and unseen. Help her to see you, know you, and hear your voice. Open her eyes! Help her to see that you can take her pain, work, and imperfections. She is very vulnerable; protect her. Let her know she is ultimately protected. Help her to rid herself of herself and know you—whatever it takes, Lord.

Comfort
"And He who sits on the throne said, 'Behold, I am making all things new'" (Revelation 21:5a, NASB).

Discussion Questions
1. Describe your most significant relationship to date.
2. Describe your view of God. Who do you say God is? What does the Bible say when you read through the different Psalms? What do you believe about the Bible?
3. Why do you suppose God allows trauma to happen? Do you believe He tests individuals? Why?
4. What does it mean when people say, "God doesn't give us anything more than we can handle?" Is there biblical truth in that? Look up Romans 8:26-38 and John 8:12.
5. Have you ever gotten caught up in yourself? What are some examples of times this has happened?
6. How do you feel about the analogy of the wolf? Who is the unseen predator in the main character's life, and how is he like the other wolves? Has this unseen predator ever come after you? How?
7. What things/people do you cling rather than placing your trust in God? Do you hold anything, your children, your favorite past-time, your emotions, your drinking, your marriage relationship or friendships back from Him, fearing you might lose everything?

WOLF #5

"Stay alert! Watch out for your great enemy, the devil. He prowls around like a roaring lion, looking for someone to devour" (1 Peter 5:8, NLT).

I knew what it was like to be foolish, seek danger, and take risks. I'd looked death in the face, seen my life flash before my eyes, and experienced the loss, regret, and harmful consequences of my own poor choices. By sixteen, I certainly knew better, but there I was . . . alone in Billings, Montana after the state basketball championship. It was 11:00 at night. I thought I had a place to stay, but I didn't. When my plan fell through, I had gone to a friend's penthouse. My friend, who was also in high school, had let me come up to his brother's room (wolf number two—before "the date rape incident"). The brothers nanny arrived and informed me that I had to go. I hadn't really intended on staying anyway, but I didn't know where else to go. So I was alone. I had no money, no cell phone, and no friends to take me in in this strange big city. I borrowed money from the brother and left to walk the streets downtown, looking for the bus station.

On my way, a small, older gentlemen dressed in many layers of worn clothing approached me and asked me where I was headed. For some reason, I wasn't afraid of him, so I told him. He told me I shouldn't be alone down there. I remember thinking sarcastically, *Really? A sixteen-year-old girl on the streets of the biggest city in Montana in the middle of the night?* I was scared—but not of this man. He led me to the red, white, and blue Greyhound sign; walked in behind me; and stayed in the waiting room until my bus arrived hours later. I was grateful for his presence, as the waiting area was filled with people from all walks of life—people of the likes I hadn't encountered before. I was very relieved to be headed home when I got on that bus. I didn't really think much of the old man other than that he was a nice person who helped me out.

Also during my sophomore year, I flew to Seattle with a good friend. We had convinced our parents that we had made all the necessary arrangements. We hadn't. We had a quasi-plan for what we mature young women would do upon our arrival in the metropolis of Seattle. We had the latest issue of *Cosmopolitan*. We had visions of Richard Gere and big-city living in our heads. We had a room to stay in on the U of W campus—a boys' dorm that was vacant during their spring break session. We arrived to a quiet campus—not totally vacant, but vacant enough for us to spend the night without anyone really noticing us. We had to carefully negotiate the bathroom situation, as there were only supposed to be college-age men using the one on our floor.

We navigated our way through the local eateries and shopping centers. One day, we realized that a man was following us. He stood outside each shop we entered, and we noticed him travelling behind us as we explored. He was not shy in his perusal. He was actually quite bold. Despite the fact we considered ourselves quite worldly, confident, and mature, we were scared. We darted into a local restaurant at one point, not realizing it was filled with only African-Americans. We stuck out like sore thumbs. Everyone stared. No one seemed to want to tell us to leave, so despite our discomfort, we stayed. When the coast was clear, we made our escape back to the safety of our dorm room—another close call.

This was this same year that I found myself at a college party in the valley outside of Missoula. It was late at night, and it had taken a very long time to find the house. I was with a group of three other high school girls who had heard about this party. We were energized about being invited to a college party. It was in full swing when we arrived, complete with kegs and lots of college football players. We didn't know anybody, but we had no problem joining in on the fun. We somehow wound up in a back room of the house that gradually began to fill up with very large, very intoxicated linemen. They were having fun, but our fun turned sour as they began making innuendos about our presence there. The door was closed behind them, and we quickly realized that our adventure could be going very wrong. I looked up into the faces of these men and suddenly recognized one of them. He was a family friend of one of my close childhood girlfriends. When I asked if he was the guy I had remembered, he looked very surprised and said he was. His entire demeanor changed when I began talking about our mutual friend. He softened and immediately settled everyone in the room down. We were let out and left the house immediately, thanking our lucky stars that nothing had happened.

The truth is that I had been surrounded by scary episodes throughout high school. I had grown tired of the lack of boundaries and the so-called excitement of always trying some dangerous new thing, especially as I realized how much danger could hurt. I think I sought out the danger as much to be rescued as for the adventure—maybe more. I thought being married would finally make me feel safe—give me the security and protection I'd been searching for—but I felt surrounded once again by circumstances that I had for the most part brought on myself.

I was living dangerously close to the edge, as I was knee-deep in schoolwork from my job, my master's degree program, and the National Board Certification; a rigorous running routine; and all the duties and responsibilities that come with being a mother, wife, and friend. I was spread so thin, I wasn't really good at anything at that time, but I was sure trying.

I was also—deep down—trying to be a good Christian. I thought I knew what that meant. It was like I had all this cargo tied to my hips and heart. I carried it around with me wherever I went. Sometimes it seemed more than I could carry alone. I longed for companionship—family—a wiser, older woman to speak to my heart and help me carry the load. I had once again started looking for someone to rescue me—to make me feel safe.

I was also trying to fill my life with accomplishments. Getting my marathon-finisher medal didn't complete me. It was nice, but I still felt the emptiness—the internal ache. I was accepted as a fellow in the master's degree program I had desperately wanted, but I didn't feel like a fellow. I felt more like an outcast, not having much more energy to expend. It was an honor, but it didn't complete the me I was looking to find.

I experienced disappointment, too. I had missed passing my National Board Certification by two points, which meant another year of work on the grueling end-product. I applied yet again for a job at a closer elementary school, but I didn't get it. I wanted so desperately to be closer to my third and neediest child, Philip, for the after-school hours. It seemed so unfair. I cried and really pouted over not getting what I thought I needed and deserved.

I became bitter and whiny. When I spoke with my girlfriends, I was often proud and thoughtless. I was really all about me—not a lot of fun to be around. I could tell my tone and manner were off. I could even tell I was putting people off. My communications at my job went sour, so I quit trying to talk to people. I began to really isolate, leaving work as soon as possible so I could run off the stress of the day. I'd jump immediately into my routine of preparing dinner, showering, and grabbing a little sleep before rising at 2:00 or 3:00 a.m. to write and work on my school work. I had truly set myself up for a crisis.

If it sounds like I am making excuses for myself, I suppose I am. Weighing out the circumstances with my ability to manage demonstrates a clear miscalculation on my part. I thought I had everything under control—managed. I was sure I had everything under my thumb. In my mind, it was just everyone else who had the problem.

*   *   *

I got called for jury duty. Jury duty was an interesting process and a welcome reprieve from such a difficult year of teaching. In a room full of more than sixty people, there were many excuses for needing or wanting to be let out of jury duty. From planned ski vacations to having to attend a separate court date, one after another, folks raised their hands. I was a teacher with a classroom full of children hoping to see my face each day instead of the substitute, but I didn't raise my hand to share that one. I mentioned that I knew one of the police officers who could be called in as a witness, but I only knew him socially. I didn't raise my hand to share that I had personal experience with a date-rape drug when that was mentioned in the court proceedings. To share that in front of all those people would have been extremely humiliating, and I didn't feel that it would affect my ability to be a fair juror. And it didn't—but it sure did a number on me emotionally.

I listened to the details and testimony, and I observed evidence for several days. All of it served as clear reminders to my own painful history. I was in over my head. In retrospect, I should have requested a meeting with the judge just to share how taxing this was, but I don't think he would have let me out of the proceedings. I was a fair juror, seeing clearly what had happened. On the inside, though, I was about to crumble. There was no backbone for the tub of goo I was feeling rise to the surface. It was becoming harder and harder to hold things together.

About that time, Russ and I began to socialize outside our regular circle. I think we had intended to reach out to the people around us, wanting to *be* the church, not just *go* to church. We invited people over for campfires in our backyard. We had parties. We shared card games. We did a lot of entertaining, thinking we were reaching out. We were unprepared and unprotected from the wolves visiting our home, however. We were unaware that they'd been hunting us, waiting for the perfect opportunity, and we simply—perhaps naively—opened the gate and let them in. Like when I was alone in Billings, like when my girlfriends and I went to that college party, like so many times before, I should have known better, but I was oblivious to the danger that lurked, stalked, and eventually walked right in my front door. One wolf in particular went for the throat.

Personal attention can be exciting—exhilarating. It can be like a physical drug, and if taken often enough, it is difficult to disengage from or give up. I was given lots of attention during this time by a wolf. He wasn't the offensive, slobbering, snarling type of wolf that one might expect. No, Rick observed what was going on in our home and our lives. He was sly and cunning. He had intimate knowledge of what was transpiring between my husband and me, because I let him in. I put my trust in him. I confided. I shared my heart with a man outside of my marriage. He waited for opportune times to come and speak with me; I sought his attention. It was like a drug for a heart so broken and empty. I couldn't get enough of it, and he saw clearly how vulnerable I was. The Internet provided a very convenient means to seek out this attention and receive it. I vented, dreamed, despaired, and engaged with this man. Meanwhile, my husband and I grew more and more apart.

I tried to tell my husband. I told him exactly how forward Rick had been. He had even made comments about my physical attributes in front of my husband, and there had been no repercussions from Russ. I told him that he had placed his hand on my leg suggestively at one of our fires. Russ's response to me was, painfully, "Then maybe you should try it . . . just have an affair with him." I swallowed these events with difficulty, digesting what I must mean to my husband: nothing. I would not be protected or even persuaded to be careful—nothing.

*   *   *

I began running more and eating less. I couldn't eat . . . I couldn't feed myself. Internally, I felt that I could no longer support or help myself. Food or anything good to do for myself felt wrong, as I knew just how bad I was. I knew what I was doing was wrong. I hated it. I hated me. I told my three dearest friends about the initial conversations with the wolf-Rick. I told them about his flirtatious behavior. I told them about my mixed feelings for my husband. I tried to convey that I was about to sink, not swim.

I looked at my children and wanted to vomit from the guilt. I looked at my parents and wanted to hide. I looked at myself in the mirror and became fixated on my appearance. I looked at my husband, and I trembled with restlessness and fear. I knew I could not function much longer in this state.

Rick sought out a deeper relationship. He told me he had fallen in love. I looked at him and didn't know who he was. I even hated things about him—especially his treatment of small children around us. He was clearly not a man seeking God's heart. He was clearly involved with me for one reason—the hope of future intimacy. He was clearly someone who would take me further away from God, Russ, and my children. He didn't care if he destroyed everything I loved. He spoke of inconsequential things—things I don't even recall—and at the time, I wondered what in the hell I was doing.

While showering after a long run one day, I looked down to discover my necklace on the shower floor, wrapped around my toes. I always wore the same silver cross necklace. I never took it off. It was always there; even when I dressed up to go out, I would keep it on. It was a bit like my relationship with Christ. I always had it on, but I wasn't always aware of it. I knew it was there when I thought about it, but I wasn't walking out into each day remembering it around my neck. It had lost its significance. And so my relationship with Christ was ornamental. I didn't go out into the world armed with my faith. I wasn't even aware anymore that I had it. I stared at the necklace. I hadn't taken it off; I hadn't even touched the clasp. I picked it up and looked at it. Everything, including the clasp, was still intact—still working. I slowly opened it back up and closed it. It dawned on me that this little sign was so fitting. My faith—whatever that was—had fallen, too.

I saw myself for what I was—flat, empty. I saw myself as broken, but obviously, like the necklace, Jesus was still working.

I didn't see that part. I just looked at myself, and I wondered yet again what I was doing.

I shared the necklace story with Rick and told him I felt he was leading me away from everything I had once valued and cherished. I told him I didn't understand my own behavior. There was no way for him to counsel me, as his mind was on things that were not about my protection or well-being. His response was limited, to say the least. I couldn't see a way out of the deep mess I was in. Again, I asked myself just what I was doing with a man so dishonorable—a man who had been involved in affairs before, admittedly. He was a thief—a wolf. And yet what was I?

He continued to pursue; I responded. I tried to quit e-mailing, but another fight—or just about anything—would trigger a response. He would show up at my house when he knew Russ was out. I craved and fought the attention exactly like a drug addict. I couldn't get enough, but then I hated myself afterwards. I couldn't believe what I was doing. I felt tainted, and I was. I felt red, raw, stained—desperate—disgusting. The sin in me was taking over.

I wanted to tell Russ. I tried. I couldn't find the words. I argued with him intentionally, hoping to find a way—even in anger—to tell him. I had never been dishonest with him in the entire course of our marriage except for the deep unhappiness I felt . . . and now this. I just couldn't find a way, but I was trying. I guess I really wanted him, a man I had loved—or so I thought—to just notice I was dying.

Shelly Blank

Father God,
*   You make intercession for us with groaning that cannot be*
expressed in words; make intercession for her. Wrap your loving
arms around this family and this woman. Heal them in the only
way that can be done—your way.

Comfort

"O Lord, you have examined my heart and know everything
about me. You know when I sit down or stand up. You know my
thoughts even when I'm far away" (Psalm 139:1-2, NLT).

Discussion Questions

1. What does it mean to place another person's needs ahead of
    your own? Are you very good at it?
2. Have you ever placed another person on a pedestal?
3. What are biblical grounds for divorce? Read Matthew 5:32.
4. How has the main character become like the wolves in her
    own life? Have you ever been a wolf in someone else's life?
5. Do you believe the main character can recover? How? Read
    James 1:13-16.
6. What is one form of release that you participate in? How do
    you cope? Is this healthy? How would God have us handle
    our pain?
7. Do you have words you can use to describe yourself/your
    feelings about yourself during different stages of your journey?
    Were those words true of you?

RUNNING AWAY

"Commit everything you do to the LORD. Trust him, and he will help you. He will make your innocence as clear as the dawn, and the justice of your cause will shine like the noonday sun" (Psalm 37:5-6, NLT).

I ate less, hoping Russ would just see the pain I was in. He didn't. He saw his wife getting into great shape and losing weight. I felt like that must be what determined my self-worth—my physical attributes. My sexual performance had always determined my worth with men. I hated that part of myself, yet it seemed to be the only thing of value. I kept wondering who I was and what I was doing.

"Yes. Just what in the hell are you doing?" my friend Janet wondered. She was my wise friend but was not always prone to a gentle-as-a-dove nature, at least with me. Being wise as a snake, she knew when to strike. She called in the troops, which amounted to her husband. Roy and Janet invited both Russ and I to coffee, and we wound up sitting at a park in their car, where they confronted both of us together. I sank deep into the back seat of the car, and I didn't think I could climb out. I was terrified of Russ. I was terrified of his response. I was terrified that he would go home, find this man, and kill him. I knew that neither Janet nor Roy had ever seen the darker side of Russ. I was terrified he would kill me—perhaps not with his hands, but his words.

Hence began the darkest days of my life. I pleaded with God to take me to heaven, wondering if that would indeed be my destination. I wanted to go. I begged. I thought about driving out in front of semi-trucks on the highway. I thought about sinking down into our hot tub after too many beers. I sought release, but none came. I lived and breathed the fear, questioning, and pain. All of these days were spent in the presence of our own dear children, who didn't know what was going on. It was agony pretending to be normal around them while dying on the inside. Still, they knew Mommy and Daddy were having trouble.

Russ confronted Rick and angrily told him to stay away from us. He also called his wife and relayed the story. Initially he denied our involvement, and then he admitted to portions of it and apologized. I saw a new side of him that made it even worse for me. Wolf number five was not only a thief, but also a coward. He lied to his wife while I came clean. I shared every painful detail, and the fear dissipated as I saw Russ hurt, not angry. My fresh pain came from seeing my husband so destroyed. I felt worse, not better. I still felt the wall between us and despaired that we were finished. The bad girl had destroyed my lifelong friend and companion—the good guy. What had I truly become?

I had always joked with my girlfriends about how Russ wouldn't know if a woman was flirting with him because he was always so happy-go-lucky. He was a fun-loving guy, not prone to flirtation himself—except with me. I trusted Russ in this way, like you'd trust falling backward, knowing your best friend would be there to catch you. I trusted Russ like I trusted a brick wall you could lean on if you needed the support. This implicit trust left me completely shattered when, a few days after my confession, Russ had one of his own. He had been unfaithful ten years earlier during his master's degree summer program. When I felt myself falling backwards and expected him to catch me, he wasn't there. I fell and fell.

*   *   *

I attempted to take an algebra class my freshman year in high school, but none of the material sank in. As I sat each day, staring at my teacher and the equations he had written on his chalk board, I sank deeper and deeper into my chair. He wore horn-rimmed glasses and white short-sleeved dress shirts with ties. His hair was perfectly groomed with a part on the side, and his countenance was less than warm. Faltering, I tried getting help. After barely getting by my three years in middle school math, this algebra class and this teacher were far beyond what I felt I could handle. I was intimidated, to say the least. His responses to my questions were less than cordial, and I was left with an F at the end of the course. My parents were shocked, and I was too. I had kind of coasted through school up until this point. I realized high school was a different ball game.

I went on to my sophomore year with the knowledge that I was headed for "bonehead math" with a bunch of kids I didn't typically associate with much (to put it kindly). My teacher was warm, friendly, and strict, but she knew how to teach someone as lost as me. I only skipped her class once. She made me toe the line. I managed to get through the rest of my high school math career in the shelter of her classroom. I began to get a glimpse of some of my academic ability, and due mainly to her ceaseless work with me, I graduated from high school.

When I returned to college as an adult, I managed to get all A's except for one B (in physics, which I'd been warned not to take!). As an adult learner with three children in tow and a student loan riding on my efforts, my academics were a priority. I wanted to prove to myself—and to everyone—that I, the black sheep of the family, was good, smart, and capable. Earning a fellowship to get my master's degree was huge for me. I had never dreamed that a student who once had to take remedial math classes could go on to get her master's degree. I was intimidated to say the least, but I had come too far in my academic battle to just walk away from the fellowship opportunity. I was ready to prove myself worthy and capable once again. My bachelor's degree was not enough. So I found myself rising early each morning and driving to school for my coursework. It was the summer after the horrific school year of turmoil.

One morning, I discovered a verse that Russ had left on a sticky note on my steering wheel: "Commit everything you do to the Lord. Trust Him and He will help you. He will make your innocence as clear as the dawn, and the justice of your cause shine like the noonday sun" (Psalm 37:4-5). At the time, he didn't realize—and neither did I—just how profoundly true and personal this message would be in our own lives and hearts. I never would have believed it—at least the innocence part. No matter how many counseling sessions I had attended over the years or Scriptures I read, I did not feel clean. I felt like my worth came from what I could give physically—and to someone about to turn forty, that's a frightening thing! I donned a perpetually unclean self-image. I had been dirty for years, and now to complete the ensemble, I felt like wearing a t-shirt with a huge *A* on the front. After all, I was not just dirty; I was stained.

*   *   *

Each day, I would come home and hope for respite, but home was not a refuge. Even there, I felt like running away. I couldn't get over the guilt and shame of who I was. I was worried constantly that I'd run into "him," and on occasion, I did. Everywhere I went, it seemed, I ran into reminders of what I'd done, his wife, or him. I'd be out running, and Rick would drive by, waving like a long-lost friend. Once he pulled alongside me and rolled down his window. He had e-mailed Russ and I and promised that there would be no communication from him, but of course he had lied. I ignored him.

However, the pain of Russ's confession along with my continuing confusion and poor self-image was too much for me. In a moment of weakness and frustration, I e-mailed the man and asked him what he had wanted the day he pulled alongside me. I told him I would gladly get out of a meeting if he called partly because I longed to vent my emotions with him and partly because I wanted to hear what he would have to say to me. Would he perhaps apologize? Thankfully, his wife retrieved the e-mail and sent it directly to Russ, which really landed me in the hot seat again. The man, of course, denied the truth, while I received very firm and direct communication from my husband and my best friend. There would be absolutely no further communication tolerated with this man. It was time to make a decision about what I was going to do with my life. Actions would speak louder than words. I wasn't sure why I acted the way I acted and did the things I did. I wasn't sure I could trust myself. I knew I loved my children, and I knew I wanted desperately to save our family. I felt totally lost—isolated. I was drowning. I wanted to die. I couldn't forgive myself. Over and over in life, I felt like I just kept failing, kept trying to do better—prove to everyone that I was good—but I just kept failing. I felt like there was no one to catch me this time; I'd fallen too far.

As I sat on our kitchen floor with our best knife, I was taunted by an indescribable image that kept telling me that it wouldn't matter if I was gone. Whatever it was, this image that sat on our kitchen counter, it was like nothing I'd ever encountered. It just sat there, waiting for me to do the unthinkable. I called Russ, who was out of town. I cried and told him I couldn't bear it any longer. He could say nothing that helped. I texted my friend and told her what I was considering. Her words rebounded. I was waiting to be convinced otherwise. I was waiting to be rescued, protected, and saved. I hid under our table, waiting for the tempter to leave. I asked God to come—if He was still there—to help me, because I was beyond my abilities. I was totally alone.

I moved to our couch. Then calm suddenly poured over me. I had an exact image in my head of a man kneeling next to me. I thought I had gone crazy, loony, nuts—checked out! Yep. In fact, I knew I had, but there was no denying the peace washing over me. I knew that nothing had changed in my circumstances. I knew what I was, but I also knew I would not take my own life because of it. There was something there in that room with me that cared for me. The garbage, the mess, the dirt—it was all still there. But there was something to hold on to—my children, the fact that my husband was willing to forgive, and the fact that he still loved me and did not view me as dirty. But how did he see me? And how did God see me? Was it true?

Father,

You rescue us from the murky places. You set our feet on firm, solid ground. Set her feet upon those high places. Take her to where you are. Set her free. You go before her and behind her.

Set the wolves free. Help them to see that they are wolves that need you. Help her to see the wolf inside herself. Without you, we are nothing. We cannot escape your loving kindness, but we must choose it. Help her to seek it. Help her to believe.

Comfort

"For when we died with Christ we were set free from the power of sin. And since we died with Christ, we know we will also share his new life . . . So you should consider yourselves dead to sin and able to live for the glory of God through Christ Jesus" (Romans 6:7-8, 11, NLT).

Discussion Questions

1. What are your feelings about the prayers? What do you believe about prayer? Read Luke 18:1-8.
2. Why do you think victims of abuse struggle so much with feelings of low self—worth? How can this be overcome? Look up Romans 6:7-8, 11 and Romans 8:1.
3. What was your reaction to the images in the main character's house? Do you believe we're in a spiritual battle?
4. Do you really believe that our innocence can be made as clear as the dawn? What would it take for you to believe, if you do not?
5. Are you able to identify anything that you truly want now? What would you do if given a day to do anything?
6. When a person commits adultery, it can be in the heart as well as in action. What things do you need to hear from another person who has survived? What specific questions do you have? How can God answer them?

STRATEGY—THE BIG FIX

"For our struggle is not against flesh and blood, but against the rulers, against the authorities, against the powers of this dark world and against the spiritual forces of evil in the heavenly realms" (Ephesians 6:12, NIV).

I secretly love office supply stores. (The secret is out!) I love organization. I love sticky notes and the perfect pen. I am happiest when I have a plan and am organized. If you want to set me back a few paces, see what happens when I can't find something that is supposed to be in its rightful place. I guess this attitude displays some sort of medical condition—OCD, or whatever—but I am happy with my own labels . . . especially color-coded ones!

I get up early almost every morning and do a load of laundry. It's kind of a rule in my house. I cannot start the day without getting something clean. There you have it. Part of it is because I have raised (and am not done yet) three children who absolutely know how to get a lot of clothing dirty, and they believe towels must only be used once. The other part of it is because I simply like routine and find comfort in having a plan. I also find comfort in getting the work done first so I can play and rest later.

As an adult professional, organization really helps me set boundaries between work and home. When I am organized at work, it prepares me in such a way that I can leave without bringing home a lot of extra prep work. I have never really bought into the myth that in order to be a good teacher, you have to stay at school until 5:00 past your contract day. There are some schools of thought that argue this as a necessary requirement for the most dedicated of our profession. However, I learned from a few teachers that the secret of a happy teacher is a well-prepared teacher. I don't function well running behind all the time; therefore, I set myself up to succeed. I have learned that even if I don't get to the plan in the day-to-day business of teaching—or even if the plan goes differently than I expected, which happens often in education—at least I've been prepared enough to be flexible. I can change things up instead of always catching up. I find I'm a healthier individual this way and am able to walk out the school door and take care of my personal business, like family.

After all of the trauma and failure in my personal business, though, I began washing and cleaning and cooking and trying my very best to make up for the lost time and stabilize the chaos. I forgave my husband. He forgave me. We began a process of healing. That was a good label for where we were. We had always been very good friends. Our friendship helped, but what got us through was that each of us sought after God. Individually, we made the decision to turn directly away from what we knew to be the wrong route, and we turned to face Him. We kind of got a little crazy—possessive crazy, romantic crazy, annoyingly crazy. But we began to learn about healing. We practiced doing a lot of things—or I did. My husband was mostly a free man.

This kind of bothered me like an itch that I couldn't quite find to scratch. Russ had laid everything out and was now free—apparently healed. He had waited ten years to do it, but it was done. And now he was just plain happy. At first, I was so relieved to be forgiven and to see this new, free side of him that I just didn't care about the garbage. I had a husband who was praying over me—with me—and reading his Bible. It was great. We went away together and spent time and money healing our marriage. We went into a little debt healing our marriage, but as our good friend said, "It is cheaper than a divorce." So we played together, laughed, prayed, took classes, ate, drank, and tried to reconnect, recommit, and heal.

Russ was extremely gentle—never harsh. He was literally a different man. He took the time to listen to me, and he actually seemed to hear me. He spent hours just holding me while I cried. I would wake up crying and go to sleep crying some days. In the middle of the day, while teaching, tears would well up, but I would feel so relieved to have come through the worst. Songs and Scripture would cause tears. Actually, just about anything would cause tears. More often, during this time, they were tears of happiness, but there was a lot of sorrow.

I remember when Russ took me away for a weekend. In our hotel room, he brought out a bucket of warm water, and he knelt before me. He gently washed my feet. My heart and soul were still searching, but I knew I loved this man. He was doing everything he knew how to do. It was sweet and pure and amazingly wonderful, but it did not make me feel clean. I worked so hard to be healed. I wanted to be cured of this enemy: dirt. No matter how clean my house was or how many verses I memorized and internalized, I couldn't quite get rid of it. It just wasn't coming fast enough.

*   *   *

I memorized Scripture for each difficult time of the day. It was actually a really effective way for me to memorize. As I began to memorize, more and more verses would come for different times of the day. Philippians 4:13 was for 4:13 in the afternoon, when I felt like crashing. I'd go for a run, remembering, "I can do all things through [Christ] who strengthens me" (NASB). Proverbs 4:23 comforted me during my run, guarding my heart from disturbing thoughts and reminding me that I was guarded by God and I didn't need to fear being seen by Rick, which up until then would make me feel naked and exposed after being involved with someone who I was really beginning to understand, only spelled destruction. It sounds silly, but it helped. Then as I read more, Philippians 3:12-14 became another favorite: "I don't mean to say that I have already achieved these things or that I have already reached perfection! But I keep working toward that day when I will finally be all that Christ Jesus saved me for and wants me to be. No, dear brothers and sisters, I am still not all I should be, but I am focusing all my energies on this one thing: Forgetting the past and looking forward to what lies ahead, I strain to reach the end of the race and receive the prize for which God, through Christ Jesus, is calling us up to heaven" (NLT). I strained to reach Him. Still, somehow, I felt like I just wasn't getting there.

I memorized Philippians 1:6b: "He who began a good work in you will carry it on to completion until the day of Christ Jesus" (NIV). I ached as I wondered when that day would come. I clung to Romans 8:1: "Therefore, there is now no condemnation for those who are in Christ Jesus" (NIV). But was I truly in? Did I really believe it? How could I not be condemned with everything I had done? I put my family on the line. I had always been a sinner. In my mind, I always would be. I just couldn't shake it.

As I pursued God, I began to understand new things about sin, though. I read about our sinful nature and that sin is actually a noun that can be removed from us through the blood of Christ. I considered, though, what happens when it comes back. I had a severe internal battle going on. Why did my feelings of low self-worth always haunt me? I felt so much guilt—guilt about not getting to read my Bible; about feeling angry with Russ, who seemed to be so good now; and guilt about eating. I realized I was still afraid to eat. I knew something was still not quite right within me.

I suffered a severe setback when I learned I had a pelvic fracture. It was caused by overuse—running too much—and the early stages of osteoporosis. I had to quit running. I had to start teaching second-graders in a wheelchair. I was on crutches or in a wheelchair for eight weeks to immobilize the pelvis. For someone addicted to running, it was torturous, and being immobilized did nothing for my self-worth or healing. I read more and more about God and healing. I felt like He was literally testing me beyond my limit. The truth was that I couldn't run to escape anymore. I had to directly face my pain.

In all this time, I couldn't tell my parents or anyone in my family what was going on. It was awful trying to maintain a façade, but I couldn't face any more judgment. I couldn't deal with their reaction—the family gossip that would ensue and the feelings of inadequacy. I was scared of what would happen to me if they knew and how I would handle it. After all, I was handling everything by trying to control everything, and once they knew, there would be no controlling anything.

I finally passed my National Board Certification, and I earned my master's degree. I could feel things wrapping up, and I could finally see God changing things within me. I began to see my students differently. For one thing, in a wheelchair, I saw them at eye level, and for another, I began to see how much of a gift each little one was. It was no longer just about the mental challenge of teaching them well and getting them to learn. It became much more about tending to their hearts as much as I could. I was beginning to feel like I could act as God's hands and feet. I began praying with my friends often before work. I could vent with these ladies about my struggles. I could literally say anything with them and with my friend, Janet, and receive no judgment. That was essential. I wanted to get to a place where I would no longer need to talk about all of this, though. I wanted all of it behind me. I wanted to push it under the rug. I wanted to wrap it up and move on.

*   *   *

My girlfriends have a way of being tough but gentle with me. I have to say that I will be eternally grateful to each of them for the toughness they have displayed in my life. Each one fulfills a different role, and I wouldn't trade any of them—even when they've had to say painfully hard things to my face. They confronted me on tough issues, like my weight: "How much do you weigh? Did you eat? You have a problem." And they didn't let me hide or wallow in self-pity: "Everyone has crap they have to deal with—you're not the only one. Talk to a counselor. You have to deal with this!"

I didn't want to dive back into the murky pit. I wanted to move on and be happy. My friends kept me moving on—moving forward. They held me accountable. I didn't always see eye to eye with them, and I certainly didn't always like what they had to say. But I am grateful now for their persistence. And I knew I still had issues. I *wanted* to be happy if I ate an ice cream sundae and not face a guilt trip at bedtime. I had an ideal weight in my head—you know, a certain number I had to stay below or I'd freak out. The truth is that on any given day, my weight would fluctuate three to five pounds, but if I got even close to that number, I'd freak out and strategize my next workout and day of eating. I did eat. I never stopped eating; I just ate less. My appetite has always been sporadic. With certain workouts it grew, and on some other days it was minute.

I decided that drinking could be part of the problem. Clearly, my body was never great at handling alcohol, and everything really bad in my life—or nearly everything—had involved alcohol. Even Russ's deal with the other woman, it turns out, had been as a result of too much to drink. My deal had started with it and many others in my life had at least an element of alcohol. It was a factor, I decided, I should try and clear out. I gave it a half-hearted effort to no avail. At least, I reasoned, I was trying to do the right things and use wisdom.

During this time, Russ and I took a class at church about the life of Christ. Jesus told a story in the book of Matthew about the Pharisees who were all about keeping the outside of the cup (their outward appearance) clean while the inside (their hearts) was unclean. Their hearts were filled with impure thoughts and feelings that would then dictate their actions. I began to sense an undercurrent in my life—in *our* lives. Maybe that was what Russ and I were doing—scrubbing the outside of the cup. I began to realize we still had issues that needed clearing up, but I was afraid of the difficult journey we'd face if we decided to drag out all our baggage. Some of our closest friends told us—and we agreed—

that everyone has junk in their trunk. So why couldn't I move on? I knew I was saved. I knew I was forgiven and even healed. What exactly was my problem? Maybe that junk in the trunk needed to be cleared out. Maybe I needed to clean out the inside of the cup. I was just so tired of dealing with the drama and pain.

There were periods of time when Russ was extremely quiet or extremely possessive. Possessiveness, in my mind, was natural, but sometimes it bothered me. Then it bothered me that it bothered me. I wanted him to want me, but at times, I still felt I needed freedom and escape. I needed to get away. I still wanted to run away from the troubled feelings in my heart. I was still confused about how I had gotten involved with someone outside my family and how I could put another family at risk. I was confused about how sometimes I still craved attention. Why? What was that all about? I hated that I craved attention. I hated parts of myself, my personality, and my character: competitiveness, pride, extreme shame, guilt, anger, and selfishness. As usual, I wanted these areas fixed right away.

My friends still bugged me about my eating, so I finally stopped in my school counselor's office one day and just asked her some pointed questions. "What if I am afraid to eat sometimes? What if I go to bed and feel guilty for eating something? What would be the normal result of these circumstances in a marriage?" I think I had her overwhelmed; she had never heard my story. I just dumped these loaded questions in her lap and asked for an opinion. "Should I maybe seek help?" I am sure I heard her thinking, *Uh, yeah, dum-dum.* After all, how could an intelligent, grown-up woman be so flipping messed up? But she was kind and professional and recommended I get some help.

*   *   *

Russ and I offered to help out in the marriage ministry at our church. I kind of found that amusing—us helping others with their marriages! But our hearts really went out for others who were struggling with turbulence or even nose-dives in their relationships. Also, as teachers, we could clearly see the toll that divorce takes on children. We hoped that sharing our own experiences and walking beside other couples might help prevent the children in their homes from the pain of divorce. We felt we had come through a difficult time that might enable us to serve in this way.

During our struggles, we took some classes at church that helped us persevere and grow closer to each other and to God, and we got to know the marriage pastor. He was younger than us but smarter. That was kind of irritating. After all, how could a younger person know more than us older, wiser people? That wasn't the only irony that crossed my mind, though. How could I—a Christian person—be so messed up? How could Christian people do the things that Russ and I had done? Why didn't Christianity work?

As the Lord continued to heal our marriage and we reached out to help others, I found I still had a lot of anxiety. I was very worried about running into wolf number five. Mostly I was afraid of how I would handle it. And I was mostly afraid because I still had unresolved feelings. I wanted closure. I wanted to tell him off—but I knew that was not what God or Russ would want. I was also very nervous about running into his wife. In my mind, I believed I had hurt her tremendously. I had betrayed her and her family by getting involved with her husband in any kind of a relationship. I didn't know if she would boldly confront me in public. I wanted to protect my children—and hers—from such embarrassment. I had apologized to her, but somehow it just didn't seem settled. Strange things happened that made me wonder.

Our daughter's car window was smashed out one night while it sat in front of our house. During the day, I watched older people walk around all the glass in the street. I realized I should clean it up, and I headed out to take care of it. While I was sweeping and cleaning, "he" appeared and began talking to me. I was incredulous. Of course he knew Russ was not at home. He asked if my daughter was okay. My internal rage hit the boiling-over point. It had been so long since I had spoken or communicated with him, and all the pent-up anger was right in front of me. I was seething at this man. I asked him, "Why are you talking to me?" I reminded him that he had promised my husband never to talk to me. He responded with some lame excuse that he was just concerned, that we had had enough time, that we would continue to live in the same community, and blah, blah, blah. I knew that if I gave this man one inch, he would take a mile. I told him he was not a man of honor and that I wanted him far, far away from me. We walked away from each other, and I crumbled inside my front door.

Russ came home that night to a trembling, shaking, and practically hysterical wife. I hated the man. I realized I hated myself still. I told him everything about the encounter. My husband retaliated. He went to this man's house and hit him repeatedly. I was terrified Russ would kill him. When he came home, he told me what he had done. It was like the drama became a full-blown, dreaded soap opera—a nightmare!

The police were called. I imagined my husband being arrested—rightfully—and our life as we knew it ending. But the police didn't arrest Russ. They did tell both of us to call them if he ever approached us again. They asked for the condensed version of our story. I shared through tears and trembling that I had seen him wave when he drove by slowly. I had felt his stare. It made me feel like a piece of meat with a hungry wolf. The police officer shared that this man had denied approaching me at first and then changed his story. Once again, I saw him for the coward that he was. I was seeking help. I was trying to heal. What was *his* problem? I knew it would not be the last time I ran into him. I needed strategies to cope. And I needed my husband to heal as well. He could not go on with anger just below the surface. Something had to give. It was clear that we were not through the crisis; there was much work in our hearts yet to be done, and I was not yet safe.

Heavenly Father,
   Make it plain. Make it apparent. Let the truth and the knowledge of who you are sink in deep. Make yourself known to her. Make yourself known to Russ. Help him to heal and seek you first. Help him to release his feelings of control over certain emotions. Heal the wolves. Teach them to repent.
   Amen.

Comfort

"I will sprinkle clean water on you, and you will be clean; I will cleanse you from all your impurities and from all your idols. I will give you a new heart and put a new spirit in you; I will remove from you your heart of stone and give you a heart of flesh. And I will put my Spirit in you and move you to follow my decrees and be careful to keep my laws" (Ezekiel 36:25-27, NIV).

Discussion Questions

1. Who is protecting the main character? What does protection mean? Why do you think she still doesn't feel safe? Do you feel safe?

2. How does the main character view God? Read Matthew 23:25-26. "Washing the outside of the cup" means trying to follow rules and look good on the outside. How has this worked for her so far? Do you find yourself doing this? Read Galatians 3:21.

3. How do people cope with anger? Are anger and contempt the same thing? What happens when you hold on to anger? Is that okay in our culture? Does your heart truly long for reconciliation? Read Ephesians 4:26-32 and Matthew 5:38-48.

4. How do we truly forgive? Can the main character forgive herself? What is holding her back? Read Psalm 37.

5. What does it mean to be saved? John 10:10 reads, "I have come that they may have life, and have it to the full" (NIV). Do you have life to the full?

6. Who do you really believe God says you are? What do you honestly and frankly believe about God? Take time to think about what His words mean to you in John 8:42-47, 1 Corinthians 13, 1 Peter 2, 2 Peter 1:1-15, 1 John 3:1-5, 1 John 5, and Colossians 3:1.

COUNSELING

"Above all else, guard your heart, for it is the wellspring of life" (Proverbs 4:23, NIV).

In middle school, I went to our school counselor. She had a cozy little office with a couch and her desk. I remember feeling compelled to talk to her. She was pretty, smart, and spunky. I also liked her name, Toni. She questioned me about a lot of things. She expressed concern for me with my parents. We never got to the heart of my issues, though. I remember desperately wanting help but not being able to articulate my pain or my needs. It made me feel even more helpless.

As an adult, I was scared to go back to counseling. I didn't want to deal with anything or reopen anything. But as I saw Russ's temper flare in a few unpredictable circumstances and as I saw myself unable to eat, run, or function under normal circumstances at times, I finally broke down and told Russ I had to return to counseling. At least now I was hopeful I could articulate my needs. I was sure I needed strong strategies to live and breathe in the same community as this other family. *Strategies* is a teacher word that I use a lot. It applied to my circumstances, and it made sense to me that some good, wise strategies would help me recover, cope, and heal—maybe even make me feel safe.

I called our church and requested an appointment with our marriage pastor—the one who, though young, was much wiser than me. I wanted to go alone at first. I wanted to feel free to completely share my feelings without fear of hurting Russ by saying the wrong thing. Verbal vomit is more like it. I went with much anxiety. I told the whole story—every painful detail. It was a lot to absorb and rehash. My job after our first session was to identify what a wolf is and to identify that each of these men, from the time that I was little, was a wolf. This was not what I expected from counseling. I was ready for a checklist of things to do or not to do, and here I sat with a question of definition. What is a wolf? I decided a wolf was clearly a person whom I could not trust—a person who meant to hurt me, whether he viewed it that way or not—a person who sought to destroy me. Did that include this man that I'd gotten involved with? It was a question I wasn't yet ready to answer.

The next week, we discussed my faith more. I had been a Christian from a very young age. I professed that I believed in God, and I knew a lot of things about Him. I had been friends— good friends—with lots of Christians, but I had never dealt with the reality of Jesus and what His words meant. It all seemed like lofty ideals, visions, dreams, and ambitions. I had never had someone look me in the eye and ask me the hard questions about what I really and truly believed about God and His grace. The tough questions were always pooh-poohed. Intentionally or not, it isn't very often that people want to hear and then deal with your true issues. It was too touchy, too emotional, too deep, and too personal. No one wants to dive into anyone's garbage that much, but we all have it. The problem was that by avoiding it, I was left bewildered in my faith, feeling unsafe and open prey for a wolf.

This wise young pastor left me to chew on that for a week. I chewed and pretty much spit it out. I just didn't believe that whole "open prey" thing. I even ran it by my safety net of people, including Russ, who readily agreed. He was absolutely sure the man I'd been involved with was a wolf. *Of course,* I thought. *Russ would agree; he hates the man.* Even though he had forgiven him, I still thought I knew how Russ really felt about him deep down in the recesses of his heart. My girlfriends were all uncomfortable with the wolf thing like me. No one wanted to touch it with a ten-foot pole. I was very uncomfortable.

The truth was that I felt responsible for my marital failure. I was not able to accept my own vulnerability. Bewildered faith or not, I felt an overwhelming sense of guilt. I could not pardon my role in it—in any of it. I was an adult. I entered into the communication willingly. I sought it out. My system of operations had produced the expected results.

I went back to counseling with trepidation. Again I was asked to talk about what a wolf is—a person who is outside God's will. This is a person who is not acting in the way God designed him to act. His choices are according to his own will, not God's. In my logic, I surmised that since I had acted outside of God's will, wasn't I too a wolf? Yes. And so I began to understand.

We discussed forgiveness. It seemed that while I was able to forgive others, there was one wolf I would not let off the hook. Did we all deserve forgiveness? Yes. But how was that forgiveness truly possible? I was stained. I could not undo what I had done. I had made bad choices, and I hurt people.

However—and *however* is an important word here—I had turned from the current behavior and my wickedness. I had sought reconciliation. I had humbled myself and sought forgiveness. I had turned the necessary 180 degrees toward God. Now I had to learn to forgive myself, I had to learn who I was in God's eyes, and I had to allow myself to feel safe in His arms. I worked through the fact that even if I couldn't forgive myself, God would make it possible for me to do that. He would equip me for all the things I could not do alone. Part of that knowledge was tangible, and part of it was not yet a reality for me.

As we talked about my past and my yearning to feel safe, I began to understand how completely unprotected I had been in every meaningful relationship I'd had from the time that I was very young. It was another awakening discovery—a cleaning out of an old and very deep wound. This sent one sharp, stabbing pain through my heart. Then it was gone.

*   *   *

My next assignment was to allow myself to feel angry and to get angry. This was a tall order. At this point, shame dominated my emotions. It numbed me to the point that my range of other feelings on the emotional scale was about zero to one. I came home and told Russ about my new assignment. With much sarcasm, he was overjoyed. "My wife's homework is to get angry with me. Great!"

Internally, I was very afraid to get angry. I didn't know what I'd do if I released all of the anger I had toward God for allowing me to be hurt as a child, toward my parents to some degree for not protecting me (even though they couldn't have), and toward Russ. Would I return to any of them? I didn't know if I would even be a Christian. I didn't know if I could continue on as his wife. Would the people I loved be able to handle my rage? It was quite scary.

My homework was not to wallow in anger but rather to work through it with God. I did a good job on my homework. In fact, I think I would have received an A if God was handing out grades—actually, maybe an A-, because I got angry with everyone, including Him. I went on a long run by myself and really pushed myself to feel angry; it came on slowly. Somehow I had always thought my anger toward God was a secret—that He didn't really know my heart. As I got toward the end of my run with the big hill already climbed, I looked through the beautiful trees and out over the pristine lake. The sun was beginning its descent, and the colors were vibrant. The leaves were bright orange, and a deep crimson red was cast against the shadowy blues of the water and the mountains. The sun threw shades of pink and auburn into the low clouds. The sight was truly a gift, and I knew I should be thanking God. It was a highly personal moment—especially when I realized I was not feeling waves of thankfulness and gratitude. What I was feeling was anger—a deep, dark anger was welling up within me.

How could a God who was trying to give me this beautiful, picturesque scene also give me the pain from my childhood? How could a gentle, loving God allow it? I allowed myself to really ask God all these dark questions that I had always thought a good Christian would never ask—or a good daughter, wife, or mother. Why did He allow any of it? Why didn't my parents protect me as a teenager—as a child? Why didn't my husband love me enough to stand guard over my heart, mind, and body? Who would ever really love me? Was I so worthless?

I knew how very much I loved my own children. I would walk over coals or to the ends of the earth to save, help, or protect them. I treasured them. And yet I hadn't done these things. I feared losing them. I knew from all the head knowledge that God was supposed to love us even more than we love our own children, but I certainly did not feel that I was loved—or that I had been. It was a painful, excruciating realization. So then what really is the depth of love? I began to wrestle with God: Who are you? Do I even believe in You? Do you really love me? I was angry. I was not a lot of fun to live with.

Father,

She wrestles with you! Teach her the truth. Help her to accept her freedom—to see that every person can be set free. Help her to know that You have an intimate plan for her—that You love her and have never left her side. Help her know that she is Yours. Amen.

Comfort

"Then if my people who are called by my name will humble themselves and pray and seek my face and turn from their wicked ways, I will hear from heaven and will forgive their sins and restore their land" (2 Chronicles 7:14, NLT).

Discussion Questions

1. Why did the main character need to get angry with her husband and her parents? Was it necessary? Look up Ephesians 4:26-27, 31; Colossians 3:8; Matthew 7:1-12; and Isaiah 61:3.
2. Is it possible for us to get rid of these negative emotions on our own? Read Romans 7. (Pay careful attention to the truth of verses 24-25!)
3. Describe a time when you felt close to God or a time you wrestled with Him.
4. What are your thoughts on the wolf? Is this the way God intended this person to act? Read Matthew 7:13-20. What are His plans for us? Look up Jeremiah 29:11.
5. Who can condemn us? Who does? Read Matthew 8:33-35.
6. What is the main character really seeking from counseling? Can God use other people to heal our hearts? Has God ever used someone in your life to heal your heart? Is there someone safe in your life you can reach out to now?

ESCAPE

"For when we died with Christ we were set free from the power of sin. And since we died with Christ, we know we will also live with him . . . So you also should consider yourselves to be dead to the power of sin and alive to God through Christ Jesus" (Romans 6:7-8, 11, NLT).

I began to see what I wanted from counseling: freedom and protection—and not necessarily in that order. But what did *freedom* mean? I sensed it involved letting go to some degree. That part was a little scary. I had learned in life that there's a fine line between letting go and running away. Even an escape could be dangerous.

When I was young, I had many forms of escape—times when I could forget about the rest of the world. I climbed up into the arms of the willow tree. I went fishing with my dad or played in the log cabin playhouse behind our cabin in the mountains of Montana. I lay on top of my mom's huge piles of fabric, hidden away from the rest of the world, and read books or whispered secrets with my friend Janet. I played with Barbies for hours in a huge wooden Barbie dollhouse that my grandfather had built. My mom had my dad set it up on an old double bed mattress so my legs wouldn't get sore from being on the concrete floor. She was a wonderful, thoughtful mom. Even when I delivered calendars with my dad on snowy evenings just before Christmas, I could escape for a few hours. Perhaps the best escapes were the few trips we took as a family when I was young—all except one that went very wrong.

My family traveled across Montana to visit the Lewis and Clark Caverns. I was in middle school at the time and had been allowed to bring along one friend. My parents and I were traveling with one of my sisters, her husband, and their new baby. We had our suburban and a tent for sleeping. The tent was large—large enough that my friend and I shared it with my sister's family while my mom and dad slept on a mattress in the back of the suburban. It was pretty outgoing of my mother to attempt this camping expedition. She had never been much of a camper. It was exciting for me to try something new with my family. We got to the caverns, and all was well. We traveled through the great caves and explored the underworld, had dinner, and went to bed. In the middle of the night, a great wind storm hit our campsite. Our tent literally blew over. My friend and I were sent to the cinder-block restrooms while the rest of my family got into the suburban. I didn't like being alone with my friend in the bathroom, but I had no choice. Eventually the wind died down, and my sister came to retrieve us.

The second night took us down further into Montana to the picturesque areas of West Yellowstone and Yellowstone National Park. We traveled through the park and set up camp just outside of West Yellowstone. After the short previous night's sleep, we were all looking forward to some real shut-eye, as we say in Montana. However, sleep was not to come. In the middle of the night, I heard a strange sound and sat up next to my niece's playpen. My uncle motioned to be quiet with his finger to his lips, and he held up his shotgun. I was terrified! I heard a low growling noise coming from outside the tent. It became very clear very quickly that we were being inspected by a local grizzly bear.

Just outside our tent was a little cooler which contained my niece's baby bottle and formula. The bear was thirsty, and it ate not only the formula, but also most of the cooler and bottle. It brushed up against all the sides of our tent. Thinking the centermost part of the tent was the best place to avoid being slashed by his enormous claws, we scrunched up next to the playpen. I cannot say what goes through a child's mind at a time such as this, but I do remember it was unimaginable terror. I knew I was unprotected. I knew I was not safe! Eventually, the bear moved on.

On our third night, we gave up on camping and stayed in a hotel in West Yellowstone. We learned later on that just two weeks after our close call, a man was mauled to death in the very same campground where we had stayed. That made quite the impression on me.

*   *   *

As I grew into an adult, my escapes involved running, glasses of wine with friends, books, and eventually trips with my family and friends. One of my favorite escapes was a hike to the summit of what we call Mt. Hakkala in Montana. It is the mountain that is located directly across the lake from our family cabin. We have two family cabins, actually—a mountain cabin from my side of the family and a lake cabin from Russ's side. Mt. Hakkala has no trail leading to the top, and it is in grizzly country. My insides were like warm jelly as we approached the shore in the boat. We had to park the boat along the shore and tie it up while we hiked up the steep mountain with our best friends, our kids, and their attack dog, Bob. As it turned out, my fear of grizzlies was in full play that day. To say I was on high alert was to put it mildly.

We summited, exhausted but elated. We looked out over the expanse of the lake and the surrounding mountains, and we were reminded of the great beauty of the place we called our second home. It was awesome to see it from a different perspective. On our descent, we encountered a large snapping sound coming from the dense trees. I had counted on Bob the attack dog to protect me or at least alert us to any danger. Instead, he cowered behind me—behind a slim tree. It turned out to be nothing of consequence—probably a moose or an elk—but my feelings of security with Bob were suddenly and totally dashed! Still, we made it down easily and without further incident. Our escape that day had been wonderful, and I was feeling somewhat successful. For the first time since that close call with the grizzly bear back in middle school, I had stepped out of my comfort zone and explored the great outdoors, and I had survived! I loved that I had faced my fears and experienced something amazing for it.

* * *

I went back to counseling to ask the tough *why* questions and attack my fear of what the word *freedom* could possibly mean. I sat angrily in my chair, pretty detached—unfeeling except for anger. I had done my homework. I had allowed myself to feel everything I should have felt about my husband's affair. I had gotten angry about it. I had gotten angry about how he lied to me for ten years. I had gotten angry about him not protecting me. I had gotten angry with my parents for not providing what they couldn't have provided even if they tried: a safety net. I got angry with God for allowing His child—any child—to be harmed.

At this point, I was feeling very vulnerable. I felt like I was at the breaking point again, yet so much time had gone by. I couldn't believe the depth of my anger. As we talked through these questions and explored my internal fury, I realized I was also sad. I was really sad. I could label another emotion. I was overcome with sorrow. My pastor/counselor talked about Job in the Bible. He had been an innocent one. He had been like an innocent child, yet he lost everything. He suffered at the hands of Satan, yet his closest friends told him his loss must have been as a result of some sin—his fault somehow. This sounded vaguely familiar.

In the case of child sexual abuse, I knew the logic: "You were an innocent child. You didn't know any better. You couldn't control it. You didn't deserve it. You weren't bad. You were helpless." However, I felt like there was always something I had done to bring it on myself. I felt like I was somehow responsible.

I had owned it. Like Job's friends, I had always pointed the finger at myself.

My counselor then asked if I was ready to accept that the man I had been involved with was in fact a wolf—wolf number five. I saw that I had to accept it. He had pursued. Yes, I was an adult. I was capable of turning away from him, and I hadn't. He saw my vulnerability; I was weak prey. He had remained present and available. He had shown up at my door at opportune times (with huckleberry martinis when he knew I had not eaten anything). He had used convincing words—told me he had fallen and was in deep. He forced me to say the words "I love you" just to hear me say them. He had enveloped and enticed me when I was at my weakest. He had not listened to me when I shared that he would be the cause of destroying everything I loved and cherished. He was sly and persistent. He did not use claws or fangs but words, songs, and stories. Not caring that it would kill me in the end, he drew me in purely for his own pleasures. Even now when writing it, it is difficult to accept.

For some people, it is easy and plain to see. For others, it will not be. I am not casting blame. I am not weaseling out of my responsibility. I had behaved as a wolf myself! It is and was wrong. It was sin. What I had to learn is that it was a shared responsibility. Sure, I had played a huge part in it, but I cannot own his part. I cannot own all of it.

The painful reality is that there are men and women in this world who will not take care of our hearts. They do not seek God's will. They seek their own way. They may never seek God's will or His heart. They are wolves. They care for themselves. They are lost. They can destroy others if they are allowed. Some actually seek out the lost. Some are only aware of their own insatiable needs. Much like addicts, they put their own needs ahead of what God would call them to do or be. I am not casting judgment. It is not a matter of judgment, but of one's own heart and one's own relationship with Christ. The relationship with Christ is either there or it isn't—black and white.

Wolf number five, as I am comfortable writing now, acted in a way that God did not design, and Rick did not turn from it. I turned from what I knew was wrong. I chose not to stay a wolf. I chose to cease my pattern of destructive behavior. I chose God even when it meant accepting that God allowed painful, awful events to take place in my life—even when it meant I may never have answers to my questions about why those events had to take place until I get to heaven—even then.

My friend, Janet, gave me a book at this point in my counseling about another woman who had been beaten and raped repeatedly by her own father in Afghanistan. Her story was brutal. It was heart-wrenching and painful to read, yet it helped me to hear it. I saw how much worse my own life could have been. I saw that she had survived. I saw glimpses of hope in her story. I saw how God can allow everything we hold dear to disappear so that all we have is Him. We can just sit at His feet and then truly know Him. But what did it mean to know Him? Could I really *know* an invisible God? Would there be any joy in that—any redemption? I came across John 10:10 in the context of a book that I was reading for a women's study during this time. I thought a lot about what it meant to have life and have it to the full. When would I feel that full life? I wanted to experience the grace, peace, and knowledge of Him even more. Our counseling sessions were bringing it home. Russ started to attend with me.

At first, Russ was reluctant to open up about his anger. He felt he was there to help me. At first, that made me angry. I wasn't the only one with a problem, after all! He just felt like I was the only one still struggling. I tried to be gentle and point out areas in which his anger had risen to the surface. His anger would cause me to shrink—not only shrink, but also shrivel internally. I couldn't function with it. I longed for him to be completely free. I felt like he had forgiven this man in word but not in heart. I wanted to get to the place where I would know he wouldn't come uncorked in a room if this man was present. I wanted Russ to be free to forgive and to practice what Jesus had commanded:

"love your neighbor." I wanted for him what I was beginning to have myself.

We talked about what that meant. It was not about welcoming Rick back in our home, as he was still an unsafe person. It was more about Russ's heart. Could he pray for this man? Could he love him? Could *he* do this? Could he make the choice to allow God to transform him? Russ alone could never do it. But I felt that if he could make the choice to ask God to change his heart, we might stand a real chance at getting past this. If not, it could mean a long, bumpy road.

It's important to me to point out that despite everything that happened, whether or not I came through the marital storm with Russ as my husband or not, I knew I'd come through it with the best thing—my one true love, Jesus. I knew by this point that He was my only source of protection, freedom, and true salvation. But I desperately longed for healing in my marriage and for Russ to experience the love and healing I was receiving from the Lord.

Our counselor was kind enough to point out several areas in which we could both stand some redirection. We went back to Romans and Matthew in the Bible. We looked at freedom from sin. We looked at what the kingdom is. The counselor asked us to figure that out. What is the kingdom? We looked at my rule-following aptitude. I ranked high on that test but low on the heart/application survey. This was real, radical, crazy stuff! I had been through my Jesus-freak stage already in my twenties. I didn't want to go there again. It hadn't worked out so well. The counselor kept pushing us, finally asking, "What does Paul mean in Romans when he says to consider yourselves dead to sin?" (Romans 6:11) It was a heavy question with a heavy discussion. It was a lot to digest. I felt like I had just eaten a huge meal, and it was time to lie down and go to sleep.

*   *   *

I had a dream right around this time where all I could hear were the words from the end of John 10:10: "I have come that you may have life, and have it to the full." In my dream, I was running through a glistening field of wheat. The kernels of wheat were full and the tips feathery on my fingertips. I had long hair, curly and golden, similar to what it had been when I was young. I was wearing a white dress and running through the wheat, letting my fingertips brush over the tops of the wheat. I was laughing, and the sun was shining. I danced, and the white flowers in my hair stayed in place! All was right in this world. It was a good dream. I woke up with the words still running through my head and heart. It was so good that I lay in our bed, wondering, *Is this how God sees me? Is this the life I am meant to have?* It was so good, I rolled over and woke Russ. I was crying happy tears.

I didn't tell him about the dream, but I told Russ I wondered how God really sees me. I told him I wanted to know. Was it a beautiful picture, or was it the way I had always felt? Was it the picture of me always needing to stand in the creek and scrub off the years of dirt? Russ began talking and shared what he felt God's vision of me was. He shared almost verbatim what had been in my dream, including the wheat, the sun, the flowers in my hair, the white dress, and me running and dancing. The tears came down. They still do. I finally felt like I had my answer. God had spoken directly to me through the heart of my husband, who was also trying to know Him.

It may sound generic. But in that moment, the words Russ used were very close to my dream. How else could he have known those details if it wasn't for God? They were images I had never shared with Russ. It was a tangible way for God to reach me. I wanted that full life. I wanted God to show me everything about Him. I wanted His kingdom, but I wanted more than some escape. I wanted to live in the reality of it. I read that the kingdom of God is a place in which God's Word has full sway. Yes, that's what I wanted. Surely there was freedom and protection there. I walked out into that new day thinking about what that meant.

Praise You, Father. Open up Your gates! What was lost has been found. Sing a new song!

Comfort

"For I am convinced that neither death nor life, neither angels nor demons,[a] neither the present nor the future, nor any powers, neither height nor depth, nor anything else in all creation, will be able to separate us from the love of God that is in Christ Jesus our Lord" (Romans 8:38-39, NIV).

Discussion Questions

1. Is there anything we can hide from God? Read Psalm 139.
2. Are we ever justified in our lack of forgiveness of others? Who deserves to be condemned? See Matthew 7:15. What happens to us when we choose not to forgive? Is it possible to forgive? Read Colossians 3:5-15. Reflect also on what you have already learned about forgiveness in previous chapters. Is God calling you to action? Do you need to forgive someone?
3. What is the kingdom? Read John 3:3-5, Luke 17:20-32, and John 18:33-36.
4. Have you ever had a moment in which you felt God spoke to you directly? Are you comfortable in sharing it? How does that impact you today?
5. Are you able to memorize Scripture? Is it important? Is it a rule?
6. What does the law do for us? Can we follow it? What was it meant for? Refer to Romans 7.
7. Do you agree with the definition of the wolf? Who can be one? Have you been one? Are you one now?

WILD KINGDOM

"The kingdom of heaven is like a man who sowed good seed in his field. But while everyone was sleeping, his enemy came and sowed weeds among the wheat, and went away. When the wheat sprouted and formed heads, then the weeds also appeared. The owner's servants came to him and said, 'Sir, didn't you sow good seed in your field? Where then did the weeds come from?' 'An enemy did this,' he replied. The servants asked him, 'Do you want us to go and pull them up?' 'No,' he answered, 'because while you are pulling the weeds, you may uproot the wheat with them'" (Matthew 13:24-29, NIV).

"From that time on Jesus began to preach, 'Repent, for the kingdom of heaven has come near'" (Matthew 4:17b, NIV).

What is the kingdom? I always thought of the kingdom as being a far-off place that I would get to someday. I thought the kingdom was heaven and that all would be right there: no common cold, no mosquitos, and saints floating from cloud to cloud, playing harps while talking with Jesus. For some reason, that version didn't sit well with me. I wanted all to be right, but I also wanted that deeply satisfying, abiding relationship that surpasses understanding in the present time. I had heard so much about it, but didn't feel I had it no matter how hard I tried!

What I wanted the kingdom to be is what Jesus said, but *now*. We live in an imperfect world with people who do less-than-perfect things—people who do not play by God's rules. I read once in Matthew that "The Kingdom of Heaven is like a treasure that a man discovered hidden in a field. In his excitement, he hid it again and sold everything he owned to get enough money to buy the field" (Matthew 13:44, NLT). Dallas Willard states in the book, the Divine Conspiracy, that "to see everything from the perspective of 'the heavens opened' is to see everything all things as they are before God." The Kingdom Among Us is simply God himself and the kingdom of beings over which his will perfectly presides-'as it is in the heavens.'" He also says, "The kingdom is simply what God is actually doing." That would be the now part for me.

It's like I have a glass of really good wine here (and I mean *now*) that I can enjoy. I am free to enjoy it—savor it. It's mine, and it was freely given to me. I can know lots about it, presently, and I can have all of it. I know what label it is, what year, what type, and how it was given to me. I get to know lots about it. Then when I get to heaven someday I will get to have the whole bottle complete with the full details of the label. I will be able to savor it and even speak to the oenologist about the wine and how it was made. He'll explain why each particular grape was chosen, why certain grapes had to wait longer than others, why certain wines taste better to me than to others, etc. You get the picture.

*　*　*

Our young counselor/pastor/friend is kind of a radical. The Holy Spirit uses him in amazing ways. He says things that put you on the edge of your seat. It makes you stop and think. I felt like I was routinely saying, "Huh? Wait. Slow down. Say that again." But if you begin reading the Bible and you stop and really think about the words Jesus said, then you realize that's what Jesus did. He caused people to stop and think. He caused them to say, "Huh?" It's a great teaching method, but it can be frustrating for the student. We went around a little frustrated for a few weeks, but we were growing, seeking, and searching God.

God's Word was coming to life in our lives. We were able to see its transforming power!

Russ and I were assigned to read Matthew, stopping each time something we read didn't sit well with us—when we didn't agree or we had an inkling of distrust in the Word. We had to reread those verses and write down our thoughts. Then we had to pray about it and find out what God was trying to teach us in that Scripture. We were told to get the context of the Scripture— dive deep! It was amazing how I could only get through a few sentences. I felt like I was in a remedial reading class—a great reading teacher, maybe, and a slow, careful student.

Our next challenge was to walk into the next day and act out Romans 6:7—being dead to sin. I decided if I was going to do this, I was going to go all the way, and then a very supernatural thing happened. I *was* pretty much dead to sin—my *old* sin. When I was confronted with the memories, which I was quite frequently, I was quite aware of it. But I could look at it and say, "Wow, that's a bunch of garbage. I'm going on without it." It's hard to describe, and it does sound freakish, crazy, and radical! But God changed my viewpoint. I had asked for His eyes. I took Him literally for once in my life, and I received! If we are going to call ourselves Christians, then why not act on the promises he laid out for us? He never says he will make us Jesus. He just promised to transform us. "Behold, I make all things new" (2 Corinthians 5:17, ASV). And so He did!

* * *

Like a switch, sin became inconsequential. It wasn't that it didn't hurt or sting. It wasn't that it didn't cause lasting results— obviously it had. It was just that I finally understood and believed with my whole heart and head that I was forgiven for mine. I walked into it. I believed I was the one wearing a white dress, not a red one. I was beginning to understand how God really did see me, and I was starting to see myself through His eyes.

I could finally wake up in the morning and know that if I didn't read my Bible, I was okay. If I didn't pray with my husband, I was okay. I knew that I would be okay if I didn't always follow the rules of Christianity. My sin problem was covered. Still, I read my Bible, and I prayed with my husband. I chose to persevere—to do things God's way. I chose to finish the race, because "God did not give us a spirit of timidity, but a spirit of power, of love and of self-discipline" (2 Timothy 1:17, NIV). I just knew deep down where it counts that my salvation was never going to be based on my ability to follow rules, my weight, my appearance, or my ability to not sin. Romans 8:1 told me that there is no condemnation for those in Christ, and I believed. I not only believed, but I also responded. I opened the door and walked in with Christ enabling me to do it. I stopped wallowing in my painful past. That was not who I was. I was never meant to be that person. I was meant to be the woman in the wheat field: delighting, running, dancing . . . free! In a difficult broken, world—yep, but free! www.sde.idaho.gov/

I realized I was truly meant to be a good wife, mother, family member, friend, and teacher. I was meant to work and act like Jesus in all my individual capacities. Had I done them perfectly? Nope. Really poorly? Yep. Would I take what I had learned and go forward? Absolutely. No one had my heart or my design. God put me in the place I was in, and I would go out in those roles with His guidance in my heart and do the best I could. Would I fail again? Yep. Would it condemn me? Nope. What would be the worst thing that could happen? I couldn't think of anything. I understood that nothing was ever going to separate me from the one who would never condemn me and who loved me despite it all.

I finally understood God's kingdom. It was rich with abundance, not obedience. I was engulfed. I took delight in learning more about God with his new eyes and fresh perspective. I was not cured of old thought patterns and habits but more alert to their creeping and lurking ways and ultimate manipulation. I read 1 John 4:4 (ASV) and understood how powerful it is to know that "he who is in you is greater than he who is in the world." This also, in turn, led me to crave His righteousness in this present world. I grieved for the things I had done—for what had been done in this world. I began to long with His heart for things to be as they should—as Jesus would have them be. I put on His heart with His power and might.

I could name things I wanted to do without guilt. I could love without boundaries. I could hope. I could help. I was protected. I was undeniably protected. I understood that I can lose nothing, because I have everything already. Actually, I understood that I can lose *everything*, because I already have *the* one and only. He really is all I need. He has an intimate, personal plan for me. I can rely on it. No matter what hazy, awful, ugly battle I face here on earth, I am presently in God's backyard. Nothing can separate me from Him. Someday I will get to ask Him about the hazy stuff, but for now I can rest in His hammock. I can play, and I finally really get it!

Praise to you, O Emmanuel!

I sing of great love for you, the risen King, the maker of the heavens and the earth, the one who sets all men free, who seeks after us, who loves us. Your love is vast, indescribable, wondrous joy. You are jealous for us. You are like a hurricane, and we, like a tree, bend beneath the weight of your love for us! I realize just how beautiful You are and how great Your affections are for us. Amen!

Comfort

"For God sees not as man sees, for man looks at the outward appearance, but the LORD looks at the heart" (1 Samuel 16:7b, NASB).

Discussion Questions

1. What is radical grace? Read Colossians 3:1 and Psalm 16:5-11.
2. Is sin inconsequential? Read Isaiah 1:18.
3. When you are in the kingdom, what is the worst thing that can happen? Read Hebrews 13:6.
4. How are we able to forgive? Read Proverbs 3:5-7. Do we need to forgive? Read Colossians 3:13, Matthew 6:14-15, and Matthew 18:21-22.
5. What is a good Christian? Read Matthew 23:25-26.
6. How are we to talk with the significant people in our lives? Read Luke 6:45. Is it possible to love them every day? Read 2 Timothy 1:17. Are the people in your live to love you every day? What is loving them? Do you believe God can equip you to truly love them? Read Philippians 3:12-14.
7. Can you identify any lies that you still believe that keep you from knowing radical grace?

SURRENDER

"Wherefore if any man is in Christ, he is a new creature: the old things are passed away; behold, they are become new. But all things are of God, who reconciled us to himself through Christ, and gave unto us the ministry of reconciliation; to wit, that God was in Christ reconciling the world unto himself, not reckoning unto them their trespasses, and having committed unto us the word of reconciliation" (2 Corinthians 5:17-19, ASV).

When a hunted animal is finally surrounded by the pack, it stops running. It stands still, often giving in to the inevitable. And so it was with me. As I read Colossians 3:1-3, I was surrounded by undeniable truth: "Since you have been raised to new life with Christ, set your sights on the realities of heaven, where Christ sits at God's right hand in the place of honor and power. Let heaven fill your thoughts. Do not think only about things down here on earth. For you died when Christ died, and your real life is hidden with Christ in God" (NLT). I stood still. Then I read the word *let* in my Bible. I thought, *Yeah . . . let*. The letting is key to surrender and realizing that when we let go of our control, things don't get out of control. Our control was just an illusion anyway. No, I hadn't started smoking pot or getting Jesus freaky—oh, maybe I had gotten Jesus freaky, but I just thought that whatever came my way, whatever garbage from this world came at me, I would let God's capable fingers take care of it. I realized He could do a better job than me. I quit trying to play God.

I realized I had to surrender my own self-loathing, self-hatred, selfishness, and pretty much my own self. I was happy to let God take it. I surrendered some large portions quickly and found, obviously, that God still has work to do in some nooks and crannies. That's good.

This process of surrendering also involved forgiveness. I had to make the choice to let God do that important work in me also—work that I was not able to do on my own. I let him take it over. I knew that if I held on to any part of that—if I reserved the right to be bitter in any way—it would only harm me or my family eventually. I had to forgive in my heart. In some areas, I have found that to be an ongoing process. I have to keep asking God to help me forgive.

Surrender also involved asking those I'd wronged for forgiveness. It seemed like I was speaking Chinese to some folks. I asked for forgiveness from some of my co-workers for walling myself off from them—disconnecting. Some honestly didn't understand why I would walk out in humility and seek forgiveness, and that was okay with me. I didn't do it to be showy or better than anyone. I wasn't being arrogant or trying to follow some rule of reconciliation. I really just wanted to respond the way I thought Jesus would. I wanted to bring healing to myself and my relationships.

I asked Rick's wife of the man I'd been seeing to forgive me. I asked God to allow her to see me genuinely and let Him take over the important work of justice and truth. I doubted she believed anything I said, but I hoped that over time she would learn the truth. I hoped she would discover the true character of the man she lived with for her own sake. This was not for my own personal satisfaction. I really was concerned for her. I learned to let God take over all things concerning them, though. When thoughts about them surfaced, I learned to leave them in the capable hands of my Father. I let go of all the stuff I couldn't even label. It just wasn't in my court anymore. It was so freeing—so healing. That portion of my life became more like a historical event rather than a life-changing tragedy. Except to take care of the hearts of my husband and children in this area, I no longer felt responsible.

I came upon a verse at this time that became my newest, most difficult memory verse. Philippians 3:12-14 reads, "I don't mean to say that I have already achieved these things or that I have already reached perfection. But I press on to possess that perfection for which Christ Jesus first possessed me. No, dear brothers and sisters, I have not achieved it, but I focus on this one thing: Forgetting the past and looking forward to what lies ahead, I press on to reach the end of the race and receive the heavenly prize for which God, through Christ Jesus, is calling us" (NLT). I focused on God and His infinite ability to wipe away the pain and sorrows I had already witnessed, and began to see him focusing my attention on deeper, worthwhile subject areas.

I asked our dear friends for forgiveness for the lies and the many opportunities for grace I had given them. I asked my parents for forgiveness for my departure from them and my lack of honesty. Then I let God take over and move me forward—and I ran.

I ran no longer to heal or kill wounds but rather to worship and work out the day's details with God. I found verses on forgiveness and protection that became a mainstay for my runs. Forgiveness is a funny thing as it creeps up on you. It becomes necessary in an instant—as soon as I open my mouth or someone opens his or hers. That's why living in a state of surrender each day is so important. I remember that I am free to live without sin—that I have that capability through Christ. As soon as something hits me, I want to look at the person through "Jesus goggles," seeing them as He does. Of course I do not do this perfectly or all the time, but a lot of the time. I was (and am) experiencing deep, profound inner joy, happiness, and peace. I keep waking up, expecting it to be gone, but I can't get away from it, nor do I want to. It turns out that once you're in, you're in! My only choice is to go deeper. Running is one way for me to do that. It gives me the time and focus I need to go deeper with God. As long as I can physically do it, I am going to get physical. It's almost like having a coach who coaches me through life's hurts as they come—and I see a lot of hurts.

* * *

I see children whose parents are angry and bitter over a divorce. They come to school lost, broken, and torn between the two people they love best. I see children who live in homes where excessive drinking and drugs are common. They come to school and are taught how bad these things are, and they are confused. I see children who are afraid, who lack conversational skills, who devote hours of time to television or video games, who may be abused, who are neglected, and who are lonely. I see them as God's creation. I get to help protect and love that creation each day, but each day I have to rely on God to do the hard work of forgiving what I see happening to these small children. I have the negative propensity, as a public school teacher, to want to bring one or two home with me each year. So far, my husband has guided me away from that and toward prayer for them.

The Bible says we get to share in God's kingdom—both in the joy of it and the sorrow. As we endure the sorrow, we develop perseverance. The sorrow I see in children comes mainly from a lack of relationship and often in their parents, a lack of forgiveness. Our culture has said that divorce won't hurt—that kids rebound. I often see the opposite. Divorce hurts. A lack of forgiveness hurts. A lack of relationship hurts. I say this not out of judgment but out of observation and experience. I am very aware that I could have been right there as a divorcee. I say it as a caution, even a plea for the protection and the hope of our children.

* * *

After all that counseling and healing, I came into a new school year with the tides of a healthy summer under my feet. I was tanned and rested. I shared some things about myself and my own summer, and then I asked my students to tell me one fabulous thing that happened to them or one fabulous thing they did over the summer. Many stories were told. It's fun getting to see all the fresh, unique faces in a crowd of little people: all different, all excited, and all wanting to learn.

One little girl raised her hand, and as I called on her, I realized her face was much different from the rest in the crowd. Hers was sad. She held her hands up and moved her hands apart. I remember her hands so well because they were still dimpled in the knuckles—a feature I just adore about young children. She explained, "My mom is over here. My dad is over here. I am in the middle. I just want us to be together." I wanted to pull her up in my lap and rock her. I felt so privileged to be in that moment with her—to be her teacher. I would get to take care of her for a year and help take care of her heart. It's the least, greatest thing I can do.

Our heavenly Father,
Hallowed be Thy name. Thy kingdom come: everywhere,
in all areas of my life. Thy will be done: not mine, on earth as
it is in heaven. Give us this day our daily bread so that we do
not worry about anything, as you will provide each day exactly
what we need. Forgive us our trespasses—all—and even those
areas that we don't know we need to ask, and help us to forgive
those who have trespassed against us. We cannot do it without
your gracious help. Lead us not into temptation, Lord, but
deliver us from evil as only you can. For thine is the kingdom
and the glory and honor forever. Amen.

Comfort

"If you try to hang on to your life, you will lose it. But if you give up your life for my sake, you will save it" (Matthew 16:25, NLT).

Discussion Questions

1. In reading John 15:1-4 who would you label as the vine? What is fruit? Do you believe that you have totally surrendered everything you presently can to God? Is there anything you still cling to? Read John 15:1-4.
2. The author is not saying that we can become Jesus but very much like Him. How do we step out into the day and act as if we are truly free from the power of sin? What does that look like? Is it possible? Read Philippians 1:6.
3. How are you able to take care of God's creation? Read Philippians 4:13. Do you have areas in which you are trying to control what you need to leave in God's hands? Make a list. Look through your Bible concordance to see if God can handle these. Read Hebrews 12 and Hebrews 2:17-18.
4. How are we to cope with the mundane activities of daily life in this imperfect world? What strategies help you: fellowship with other believers? Reading your Bible each day? Prayer?

What if you don't practice these? Have you allowed them to become rules that determine your worth with God or are they a part of your relationship? What happens when you persevere in these areas? Read Proverbs 4:23, Psalm 51:10, and Matthew 23:25-26.

5. What does your ultimate kingdom look like? Can you ask for it? Read Ephesians 2:8-10, Romans 5:4, John 14:1-4, and John 16:24. Will it be just as you expect? Read 1 Kings 8:22-56. What would saying the Lord's Prayer in your own words sound like?

6. Has this study helped you to release some of the things you were holding back and not giving to God? If so, how has it helped?

FREEDOM

"Yes, I am the vine; you are the branches. Those who remain in me, and I in them, will produce much fruit. For apart from me you can do nothing. Anyone who does not remain in me is thrown away like a useless branch and withers. Such branches are gathered into a pile to be burned. But if you remain in me and my words remain in you, you may ask for anything you want, and it will be granted!" (John 15:5-7, NLT)

My whole life I had viewed God as far away—a distant Santa Claus-type guy. I saw him as someone who cared about us—even loved us—but not someone who was in the trenches with us all the time or who would equip us right now. I had viewed heaven as a place where I would finally be at peace, but I wasn't sure I liked the idea of hopping around from one cloud to another for eternity. I had viewed prayer as a bit like a vending machine. I would drop in my prayer and hope for Cheetos, understanding that sometimes the machine might jam, I might press the wrong number combination, or the machine might send out Doublemint gum instead—not exactly predictable. I might not get what I expected, hoped for, or felt I really needed. I'd return again and again, dropping in my prayer, and hoping to get what I wanted—something to make life better. I had EES—eternal expectation syndrome. I lived in the hope that one day, I too would feel better.

Continuing my recovery and my search for a living relationship with my Savior, I read all of Romans, focusing on chapters 6-8. I felt like my head was turning on its side. I read about a new kind of freedom. Most people think of freedom as being free to do what we want, but I was discovering a freedom to *not* do what I didn't want to do. I discovered that I can be free from the power of sin through the power of Christ. I actually have a choice: to choose sin or not to choose sin. It's a simple concept but a complex reality—or is it? Perhaps *this* was the freedom I was so desperately seeking.

To grasp that I was free from the power of sin was huge, but then to learn that the law no longer held me in its power because I had died to its power when I died with Christ (Romans 7:4) was confusing. Wait a minute! That gave me great pause. I thought the law was good for us! I was a recovering rule-follower, after all. But Romans was teaching me that the law (meaning the Old Testament set of rules—the Ten Commandments) was good for us, but it didn't rule us. It taught us how to live, provided the boundaries we desperately need for life, and also showed us how completely incapable we are of being perfect. They demonstrate our total need for dependence upon God; no one can follow them here on earth without His help. "God's law was given so that all people could see how sinful they were. But as people sinned more and more, God's wonderful grace became more abundant. So just as sin ruled over all people and brought them to death, now God's wonderful grace rules instead, giving us right standing with God and resulting in eternal life through Jesus Christ our Lord" (Romans 5:20-21, NLT).

These were not new passages to me, but I woke up in my new state of surrender and began seeing the power in His words—living words that brought life and hope to me. I memorized Scripture like never before—a newly acquired skill. I had already begun attaching verses to difficult periods of the day, but God drew my attention to more and more. At 8:00 in the morning, when I needed to remember who I was in Christ, I would remember Romans 8:1: "So now there is no condemnation for those who belong to Christ Jesus" (NLT). Then at 8:28 a.m., as I started the work day, I would recall Romans 8:28: "And we know that in all things God works for the good of those who love him, who have been called according to his purpose" (NIV). I began to see the kingdom of heaven *immediately* in this imperfect world at work all around me.

While at work, throughout the day, I lined up other verses that had become very significant. At 1:06 in the afternoon, when I often grew tired with half the day left, I'd remember Philippians 1:6: "Being confident of this, that he who began a good work in you will carry it on to completion until the day of Christ Jesus" (NLT). And I clung to the promise that God was *still* at work in me. I have enjoyed discovering and collecting the time-relevant favorites (listed at the end of the book). With my new eyes, portions of the Bible took on new meaning. Memorizing Scripture has become an amazing tool in my life—a part of a winning strategy for me. It's a way of feasting on truth throughout the day.

I did other religious things, but not religiously. I met with other Christian women for Bible study regularly. I got up early often (but not every day) so I could pray and read my Bible. I prayed often (but not every day) with my husband. I often prayed before work with other women, but not every day. Russ and I joined a small group which met regularly. We met often for family devotions. I maintained relationships that were necessary for accountability and fellowship, especially with our good friends, Roy and Janet. All of this strategy has carried on—not because it is some formula for being a good Christian or because I am trying to follow some list of rules, but because I crave the relationships with Christ and people in His kingdom. I also crave His freedom for other people. Free from sin and the law, I am following my righteous desires—desires God has put in my heart! We will never arrive at Christianity, so I need to keep learning, seeking, and growing. We all do.

I remain annoyingly excited about God's kingdom! I really want everyone to know the joy and happiness I experience—especially women who have walked a similar path. Russ keeps reminding me that it's not up to me to convince people—just point. So I point them to Christ. It's so good that I have Russ to guide me, but even without him, I know I've got the best compass of all.

*   *   *

I met with a woman whose life seemed to be taking yet another unbelievable downward turn. This woman was a long-time friend, and I had already watched her lose her health, career, and home. Now she was losing her marriage. I thought of the immensity of her loss. I had no quick remedy or catchy encouragement, but I prayed, and my prayer was the best gift anyway. When I thought of her, my heart would beg God to bring a miracle. He has so many children to care for, but I know He hears. He cares, and He will answer us. He hasn't yet—at least in the way we hope for—but that doesn't mean He isn't working, and that doesn't change who He is. I don't use God like a vending machine anymore. I will wait and trust. He's a big God, and He's handling it.

As we meet and pray, my friend has begun the painstaking steps toward God—her only refuge and hope. She's utterly hopeless except for Him. We will not let the enemy win. We will pray and ask God not to allow the enemy to constrict her heart so much so that it is consumed by sadness or bitterness. Together we will focus on Jesus and His teaching, asking God to protect her and her children. What she has to overcome seems insurmountable, but it isn't. I hope that her total reliance upon God as her only savior and hope will eventually bring about a lasting joy in her life that is a witness to the world.

We talk a lot about why some of us must suffer so much, yet others seem to walk through life unscathed. God knew His children would wrestle with this question. I am brought back to Job again; his words echo some of our own conversations, past and present. He loved God. He still lost everything. What I hope my friend can learn (what I learned) is that even when we lose everything (what we see as "everything" here on earth), we gain a relationship with Christ, and we gain everything. We gain *true* salvation—not in money, houses, cars, our mate, or even our children, but in knowing Jesus Christ personally and relevantly. He loves our spouses and our children even more than we do! We gain *everything* when we surrender it all to Him. If I hold on to anything, it can only eventually be used against me. So I gladly—painfully, at times—give it all up to Him.

*   *   *

We control so little in life, but boy had I been trying. I realized I not only needed to surrender my treasures to God, but I also had to release my control to my heavenly Father. Our plans on earth may not go as we planned. We may not get to have a mansion hidden away in a deep forest with a sandy beach in front leading to a quiet lake stocked with lake trout and hilly, winding trails all around that lead directly to our best friends' homes, where we go to work, rest, eat, and share, but He knows our hearts' desires. He knows our desire for relationships, work, health, athleticism, and riches—personal details that we can trust Him with. He is working on our own intimate plan for eternity. All we have to do is ask Him and trust Him to provide while we live out our time in the present kingdom—the imperfect one.

In this present kingdom, we have access to our Father daily. Prayer is a lifeline. Through it we see more and more clearly how God hears and answers—sometimes in surprisingly clear ways and sometimes not. I like to think of God as the ultimate parent, busy in His house, taking care of all the details of life—dinner, laundry, vacuuming, cleaning up the vomit left by a child, making the house pretty, talking with my brothers and sisters. He's got it all under control and is working it all together. Meanwhile, I stand at His door, and I knock (pray). He may come right to the door and answer me—and then again, He may not at the present time. It's in His timing. He is not a vending machine for answered prayer, but a parent who knows full well that I am there, knocking, hoping, wishing, and casting burdens, sorrows, cares, worries, thoughts and questions on His doorstep. It similar to what a parent does as he or she cares for a crying infant. The parent knows the child is hungry, but he also knows she needs a diaper change and pajamas on so that when he feeds her, she can go to sleep right afterwards and rest. It's not that He is too busy for me. He hears me. He knows every detail about me. He wants me there, talking and crying out to Him. But He has a bigger plan for me than I can see or imagine at that specific time. He answers whether I hear Him or not. Sometimes I am so busy praying or doing that I miss His answer. He listens. He cares deeply. He is always there. He never leaves me, even when He doesn't answer directly. I can rest on His doorstep. I can learn to rest in His timing, voice, and care—just like a small child learns to trust a parent through his calm reactions under her pressure. My ultimate parent has got it all under control.

Russ and I are developing a plan together for our life, which may sound like it has become perfect, but is not. We would like to be in charge of that plan, but we are not, and that's good. God wants us to always be in a relationship with Him and seeking Him. This often translates as "I will come into your day and make it interesting—or not." We must be, and He wants us in relationship with Him throught the tedious everyday experiences, as well as the challenging and exciting times in our walk with Him. Either way, we are developing a plan, with His guidance, to help others survive—to be Jesus to others, as our friends were to us. Without them, we may have been allowed to self-destruct. They stuck with us. In this day and age, friendship like that is not common—sadly, even in the church.

So what does this plan look like? It is an ever-growing, every-changing strategy to live for Christ and thus far includes being free from anger (the kind you carry around and hang onto) and condemnation, being free to love, being transparent, and choosing forgiveness. We have committed to no more pretending, covering up, or insincerity. We have chosen to live in this new way rather than the old. Praise God we have chosen a new life in Christ!

Just as I struggled with forgiving myself, Russ was a little wary of the forgiveness piece at first. He still struggled with anger toward wolf number five. And I struggled with his anger. When Russ's anger flared, it used to drive me into oblivion. Feelings of shame, remorse, guilt, and fear choked me. We discovered that his anger was often rooted in fear, though. I was learning to live without fear, though, and I wanted him to be free of it as well. As we studied the Beatitudes and further on into Matthew, we discovered Jesus's teaching to be right at heart level, although confusing and even confounding at times. We learned that Jesus's message in Matthew wasn't a checklist of behaviors. We didn't have to mourn to be good Christians. *As* Christians, we *would* mourn for the effects of our sin. We would mourn over our actions, but we would no longer *wallow* in them. Sin is inconsequential except for the effects our actions had on the people here on earth. We were willing to accept that. I learned that I had to forgive those who had hurt me—even (especially!) myself. People act in ways God did not intend them to act and hurt others. That's a reason to mourn.

People get caught up in this broken world. Some dress as sheep but act like wolves. I learned that we are all capable of that, but we have a choice. We have free will. We can choose God or choose sin. When we choose God, we become a part of His Kingdom—we're in. We cannot be separated from Him! We are His children. He loves us no matter what we do, who we are, where we've been, whether we are following the rules, or whether we're clean or dirty! Russ and I saw our part in it all and surrendered ourselves to a God who wanted us more than anything.

We began really studying what Jesus said and taking on His words in a radical new way. Russ, with God's help, let go of his anger toward his neighbor. He let go and allowed God to take over that control of his heart. And when he did that, he was really free! It was strange how suddenly we saw our current garbage so clearly and how we needed to let it go. So often in our day-to-day walk, it would surface. It wasn't that we were perfected by any means, but we had the knowledge that with Jesus at our back, we actually did have the power to choose to be without sin. Our lives became defined by choices, not circumstances or feelings. We had the power to love others even when our feelings were hurt. Jesus's goggles were allowing us to see better.

*   *   *

In hindsight, we have learned seven categorically essential lessons in our recovery so far. We believe:

- We have made peace with God.
- God truly loves us.
- We are each identified as a child of God.
- We have a path marked out for us by the one and only good God.
- We have a secured future.
- We have the power within us to take on our addictions, hurts, and weird hang-ups (of which we identified several).
- We have the means to be in relationship with others through humility in the present kingdom of God.

At this point in our walk with God—our journey—we are continually amazed at how free we are. We walked into His backyard, and we never want to leave. He has changed our hearts so that we are both open to helping and serving others. We want to share His message of hope for all marriages and all broken hearts. We have begun mentoring other couples. I am leading small groups of women, and Russ is sharing his heart and wisdom in small groups of men. We have placed ourselves ready to do God's will and His work together.

Perhaps the most profound freedom I've found in my recovery is being transparent with others. And I can only do that with Jesus's help. It's essential! There is no hiding with Him—just hiding *in* Him. The hard, painful work of truth at all costs releases me from fear. Knowing there is nothing to fear is amazing! There are no words for it. I know there are wolves out there, but I am not afraid. I know I was once stained and afraid I'd never get clean enough, but I've seen the cleansing power of Jesus's blood. He's given me a choice, and I've chosen Him. Like the little girl dancing in the wheat fields in my dream, I am free. I am full of joy, and I am white as snow.

Father,

May her children see Your hands at work in their parents'
lives and in their own. May they see their parents as real people
who love God above all else and who love them unconditionally.
Help them see that their parents for these children with Your
help. Then help her to continue to fight so that one day she too
can share Paul's words from 2 Timothy 4:7 "I have fought the
good fight, I have finished the race, I have remained faithful"
(NLT). Until this race is done, help her to continue to camp out
on Your doorstep and in Your backyard. It's got a great view!
Set the readers' hearts free to see you clearly.
Set the wolves free.

Comfort

"The master was full of praise. 'Well done, my good and faithful
servant'" (Matthew 25:21a, NLT).

Discussion Questions

1. Is it necessary to put up a fight? How do we fight? Read 2
    Corinthians 10:3-
2. Is there anything you still fear? Read 1 Samuel 17:37, Psalm
    46:10, Psalm 121:1-2, and Deuteronomy 31:6.
3. Do you feel that you will receive the "well done" blessing?
    Why or why not? Read 2 Corinthians 7:9-11 and Matthew
    25:23.
4. What is a blessing? *Blessed* means "happy." Look at Matthew
    5 and the Beatitudes. They are not a checklist for Christian
    behaviors; they are an invitation to know Christ. He wanted
    any one of those sufferers—are you one?
5. Does God's Word have full sway in your life? What would
    it take for you to take Him literally? Can you walk out into
    His backyard?
6. How are we to behave when we come in contact with a wolf?
    What should be our attitude? Do you believe you can see a

wolf as a person who is not aligned with God's heart or not behaving in a way that God intends? What would it take for you to accomplish this?

7. Are you in the kingdom? Are you living life *fully* in God's kingdom?

- Do you experience peace with God? (Romans 5:1)
- Do you know that God loves you? (Romans 8:31-38)
- Do you know that you are identified as a child of God? (Ephesians 1:13)
- Do you know that your path is marked out for you by a great and good God? (Romans 8:28, Hebrews 12:1)
- Do you know that your future is secure? (2 Timothy 4:7-8)
- Do you believe that you have the power within you to take on your addictions, hurts, and hang-ups? (Ephesians 1:18-19, 2 Timothy 1:17)
- Are you in humble, transparent, accountable relationships with others? (1 John 1:5-7)

God is always waiting, ready, and seeking for us. He has his hand outstretched. Are you reaching back and resting in Him?

These are certainly not rules but predictors. Our Father loves us and wishes none of us to be lost. If you struggle with your sincere belief in one or more of these areas, ask God to teach you more about His character, and be patient! He is a parent to many. Stand at His door and knock, but also be prepared to receive—perhaps not what you expect!

You can write to the following address and share your story. The author promises to write back. All contact is confidential.
Contact Information: sblankvip@gmail.com

Daily Verses for Life

The list keeps on growing. Remember 2 Timothy 1:17, "For God did not give us a spirit of timidity, but a spirit of power, of love and of self-discipline" (NIV). Win the race!

<u>Verses that coincide with times during the day:</u>

Romans 8:1 (i.e. 8:01 a.m.)
Romans 8:28
2 Corinthians 10:4-5
John 10:10
Hebrews 12:12
Philippians 1:6
Isaiah 1:18
James 1:19 (Memory Strategy for this verse: Quick, Slow, Slow)
2 Timothy 1:17
Philippians 3:12-14
Proverbs 3:5-6
Philippians 4:8 (TNJPLAEP: True, Noble, Just, Pure, Lovely, Admirable, Excellent, Praiseworthy)
Philippians 4:13
Proverbs 4:23
Ephesians 4:29
Romans 6:7-8, 11
Matthew 6:34
Luke 6:45
Psalm 121:1-2

<u>Other favorites:</u>
Psalm 51:10
Psalm 46:10
Psalm 139
Psalm 37
Jeremiah 29:11
Deuteronomy 31:6
Isaiah 55:11
Hebrews 13:6
Matthew 28:18-20
Matthew 5
Romans 8:26
Galatians 5:1
John 15:5-7
Matthew 23:25-26
Hebrews 12
1 Peter 4
John 15:1-4
Luke 17:20-21